ABOUT THE AUTHORS

Timothy Freke and **Peter Gandy** are internationally respected scholars who have authored six books together, including the international bestseller *The Jesus Mysteries*, which was a "Book of the Year" in the prestigious *Daily Telegraph* (UK). Their other books include *Jesus and the Lost Goddess*, which was cited by Dan Brown as an inspiration for *The Da Vinci Code*; and *The Laughing Jesus*, which was critically heralded as "one of the most important books that has emerged in this infant millennium." Timothy runs seminars exploring the experience of Gnosis in the USA, Europe, and South Africa.

For more information, see **www.timothyfreke.com**.

The

GOSPEL

of the

SECOND

COMING

ALSO BY TIMOTHY FREKE AND PETER GANDY

JESUS AND THE LOST GODDESS:
The Secret Teachings of the Original Christians

THE JESUS MYSTERIES:
Was the "Original Jesus" a Pagan God?

THE LAUGHING JESUS:
Religious Lies and Gnostic Wisdom

LUCID LIVING: a book you can read
in an hour that will turn your world inside out

൜

HAY HOUSE TITLES OF RELATED INTEREST

THE DISAPPEARANCE OF THE UNIVERSE, by Gary R. Renard

THE DIVINE MATRIX • THE GOD CODE
—both books by Gregg Braden

FATHER GOD • MOTHER GOD—both books by Sylvia Browne

I WANT TO SEE JESUS IN A NEW LIGHT, by Ron Roth, Ph.D.

THE JESUS CODE, by John Randolph Price

൜

The Hay House titles above are available at your
local bookstore, or may be ordered by visiting:

Hay House USA: **www.hayhouse.com**®
Hay House Australia: **www.hayhouse.com.au**
Hay House UK: **www.hayhouse.co.uk**
Hay House South Africa: **www.hayhouse.co.za**
Hay House India: **www.hayhouse.co.in**

The GOSPEL of the SECOND COMING

TIMOTHY
FREKE

and

PETER

GANDY

Jesus is back . . .
and this time he's funny!

HAY HOUSE, INC.
Carlsbad, California • New York City
London • Sydney • Johannesburg
Vancouver • Hong Kong • New Delhi

Published and distributed in the United States by: Hay House, Inc.: www.hayhouse.com • *Published and distributed in Australia by:* Hay House Australia Pty. Ltd.: www.hayhouse.com.au • *Published and distributed in the United Kingdom by:* Hay House UK, Ltd.: www.hayhouse.co.uk • *Published and distributed in the Republic of South Africa by:* Hay House SA (Pty), Ltd.: www.hayhouse.co.za • *Distributed in Canada by:* Raincoast: www.raincoast.com • *Published in India by:* Hay House Publishers India: www.hayhouse.co.in

Cover design: Amy Rose Grigoriou

Library of Congress Cataloging-in-Publication Data

Freke, Timothy.
  The gospel of the Second Coming / Timothy Freke and Peter Gandy. -- 1st ed.
    p. cm.
  ISBN 978-1-4019-1838-5 (hardcover) -- ISBN 978-1-4019-1839-2 (tradepaper) 1.
Gnosticism. 2. Spiritual life--Gnosticism. 3. Jesus Christ--Gnostic interpretations.
I. Gandy, Peter. II. Title.
  BT1390.F73 2007
  299'.932--dc22
                                2006100716

Hardcover ISBN: 978-1-4019-1838-5
Tradepaper ISBN: 978-1-4019-1839-2

10 09 08 07   4 3 2 1
1st edition, October 2007

Printed in the United States of America

INTRODUCTION

BY PROFESSOR FAYE KINNIT,
IMMACULATA COLLEGE OF FEMINIST THEOLOGY, TEXAS

In the Gospel of Matthew, Jesus famously declares: "All that is hidden will be revealed." This prophecy would certainly seem to have been fulfilled when it comes to the history of Christianity itself. In the last few decades, the discovery and publication of a flood of early Christian texts, popularly known as "Gnostic gospels," has forced scholars to completely revise their understanding of the origins and meaning of Christianity.

In 1977 James M. Robinson and his team published *The Nag Hammadi Library,* which contained a collection of Gnostic texts discovered in Egypt in 1945. More recently, in 2006, Rodolphe Kasser, Marvin Meyer, and Gregor Wurst published the Gospel of Judas. Such "heretical" texts were suppressed by the Vatican in the fourth and fifth centuries c.e., but it has long been suspected by conspiracy theorists that copies were secretly retained in the Vatican Library.

This idea has found little favor with serious academics. In 2005, however, an archivist at the Vatican Library, known for legal reasons as "V," made contact with revisionist historians Timothy Freke and Peter Gandy and offered some startling information. V had been so impressed by Freke and Gandy's groundbreaking work on the Gnostic origins of Christianity that he decided he was morally obliged to inform them that the library had not only possessed a copy of the Gospel of Judas for centuries but also housed many other Gnostic manuscripts that endorsed their controversial ideas.

At their initial meeting, Freke and Gandy asked V to provide concrete evidence that the Vatican was in possession of unpublished

Gnostic texts. Although initially reluctant, V eventually responded by presenting them with a facsimile copy of an ancient work entitled "The Gospel of the Second Coming." It is this manuscript that's being presented to the public for the first time in this book.

Like so many Gnostic writings, this text is largely incomprehensible. Nevertheless, it has disturbing ramifications which will shock academics and Christians alike. Not only does it make the extraordinary claim that the long-awaited "Second Coming of Christ" has already happened, it also confirms the lurid speculation about Jesus's intimate relationship with Mary Magdalene.

The manuscript begins with an unintelligible inscription that scholars haven't yet deciphered. Freke and Gandy speculate that it may be a magic spell to be intoned before embarking on the study of the text as a charm against the possibility of demonic delusion. They may be right about this, because to understand the Gnostics we need to go beyond our habitual ways of seeing and look at things from a different direction.

It is an honor and a privilege to peer-review the work of Freke and Gandy and to offer my assistance in bringing this remarkable discovery to the attention of the public. *The Gospel of the Second Coming* is an incredible find, in the true sense of that overused word, which will do for Christianity what *Animal Farm* did for Communism!

DAERUOYGNIHTYREVEEVEILEBTONOD

CHAPTER 1

And so it came to pass that Jesus spoke to the twelve, saying: "I will reveal to you the mystery of mysteries, which it is my ministry to disclose. The good news that leads to eternal life. The truth that will set you free. Be not afraid when I tell you that I am not who you think I am. I am not a man of flesh and blood. In fact, I don't really exist at all. I am the fictional hero of an allegorical myth."

A great silence fell upon the disciples, and Jesus added, "I know it's a bit of a shock."

Then Peter spoke in amazement, saying, "Lord, I understand not the wisdom of your words."

And Jesus replied, "Listen up and I will reveal the astonishing truth. What I am exists far beyond this world we inhabit. Jesus is a character in a story, and I am the Author speaking through Jesus."

Peter looked gobsmacked, so the Lord explained, "I am the Creator of the story, so I am everything in the story. I am this rock and that piece of wood. Whatever you do to anyone, you do to me. Look inside yourself and I am there. Do you get it now?"

"You're saying you're God!" announced Peter enthusiastically. "I like the sound of that. It's a bit blasphemous, but extremely impressive. And as one of your close disciples, it makes me look good."

"That's just theological twaddle. I'm trying to tell you something obvious about our predicament right now," declared Jesus impatiently. "You and I are characters in a story being imagined by the Author. We don't really exist."

"Look, Lord, we'll never set up the biggest religious cult in history with this 'no one really exists' nonsense," advised Peter. "Leave the philosophy to Socrates. Think of your market. Stick with the simple parables and homey homilies: The Good Samaritan . . . you know, that sort of thing."

"But we're in a parable right now, for Heaven's sake," replied Jesus, beginning to find Peter irritating as always. "This is a fable, and we're symbolic figures in it. Understand and be astonished."

"I'm astonished, all right! I've been going along with your crazy ideas for a year now, but to be honest, I've had enough. One minute you're God, then you're just a man . . . and then you don't exist at all. Next you're going to tell me that your water-into-wine stunt was a cheap conjuring trick done with mirrors."

"Speculating about how I pulled off my miracles is a complete waste of time, because I didn't really do any miracles!"

"I'm not sure about this new direction, Jesus," complained Peter. "I like my heroes to be historical. And I like my miracles to be genuine supernatural anomalies."

"It's not a new direction; it's just the truth," insisted Jesus. "I've always referred to myself as 'the Son of Man,' which is a Semitic idiom meaning simply 'a man'—any man. It's a literary device to show that I'm an Everyman figure in a symbolic myth."

"Well, you're a lot more than that to me, Lord. As far as I'm concerned, you walk on water. Literally!"

"It's a *metaphor,* for Christ's sake!" said Jesus, unable to contain his exasperation.

Peter felt the anger of the Lord and fell into penitential silence. Finally, he said sheepishly, "I have no idea what you are talking about, Jesus. Sorry."

"Of course you don't, dear Peter," said Jesus, adopting a shepherdly tone. "You represent the foolish person in this story, which is why I gave you the name 'Peter,' meaning 'clod.' You play the part of a clod who doesn't really get it, whilst I play the lucid mouthpiece for the wisdom of the Author."

"That doesn't sound very fair," muttered Peter, a bit put out.

"Fair or unfair is irrelevant. We don't exist. We're made-up characters in a story."

"Well, what about Mary?" asked Peter petulantly. "I suppose she's real enough! You'll look pretty sad if it turns out that you've been sleeping with an imaginary woman!"

"Whoa, Peter," cautioned Jesus. "You know there's nothing about any of that in the Jesus story. At least not in the official version."

Then Mary Magdalene spoke, saying, "Yes, Lord, please do tell. I suppose that I don't really exist either? And as a woman, I find that disappointingly patriarchal."

And Jesus answered, "You're also a character in this great story. You play the part of the foolish soul who is lost in the world, searching for love in all the wrong places. But you're redeemed by the Christ and become the wise soul who listens and understands."

"I didn't understand a word of that," declared Mary, because she was usually pretty honest, although she did occasionally tell a few white lies about her past.

"You don't understand *yet*," Jesus reassured her. "But you will by the end of this gospel."

"I'm sure you're right. You're always right," conceded Mary, because she was on a bit of a guru trip with Jesus and wrongly assumed that he was infallible about everything.

"It's only because I am the voice of the Author who has the prerogative of deciding what will turn out to be right," confessed Jesus.

"So let me get this straight," said Mary. "You're saying that this is just a story."

"Bingo!" exclaimed Jesus anachronistically.

"But doesn't that make all of our adventures together completely meaningless?" asked Mary. "It all felt so important when I believed it was real. Now it seems like a bit of a damp squib."

"The opposite is the truth," replied Jesus reassuringly. "Understanding that the Jesus story is a myth reveals its true significance. You see, the Jesus story is an allegory for the spiritual journey each person must make if they are to awaken to the mystical state that the original Christians called 'Gnosis,' which means 'knowledge.'"

Then he added portentously, "And what's more, I am going to decode the allegorical meaning of the Jesus story and reveal the secret teachings of Gnosis later in this gospel. Only this time I'll mix the heavy stuff up with some witty banter to make it more entertaining for the masses."

"Wow! Secret teachings!" enthused Mary. "Sounds fantastic!"

"Sounds like flippant nonsense," complained Peter.

"This gospel will be flippant, but not *just* flippant," explained Jesus. "Satire also has a serious side, which is what makes it the highest form of wit. After all, the real literary stars of the ancient world are satirists such as Menippus and Lucian. Their hilarious rants about wandering miracle workers making a fortune out of the gullible are a hoot. So I've decided to do this new gospel in the same genre."

"Exactly how much Eucharist have you been drinking?" interrupted Peter.

"I'm sorry," replied Jesus. "I must try to watch my tendency to indulge in obscure digressions. After all, I screwed up last time by being too cryptic."

"Last time?" queried Peter.

"There I go again," said Jesus cryptically.

Peter looked as confused as Catholic theology, so the Lord comforted him, saying, "It's of no importance that you understand, Peter. I'm not speaking for your benefit, but for the reader who is reading these words. It is the reader I desire to set free. It is the reader to whom I will reveal the secrets of Gnosis."

"Who the Hell is the reader?!" asked Peter.

"A good question," said Jesus, "and one I hope the reader will ask themselves, because that question leads to Gnosis."

Then he added, "This gospel is going to demand that the reader engage deeply with the ideas I am going to explore. They'll need an open mind, because I'm going to suggest that they are also a character in a story."

"You've gone completely bonkers," concluded Peter with a disgruntled snort.

And Jesus told him straight, "It's no good arguing with me. I don't really exist."

"Do you know your problem, Jesus?" pronounced Peter pointedly. "You're obsessed by your own nonexistence. Just let yourself *be* for a moment."

Then Peter put his arm around Jesus in a blokey sort of way and suggested amicably, "Curse a couple of fig trees like you used to do in the old days. You'll feel like yourself again in no time."

And so it came to pass that the Lord pulled himself up straight, because normally he had a bit of a hunch like the Dalai Lama, and bellowed, "You're as brainless as a rock! If I'm not careful, you'll go off and found an authoritarian church based on a complete misunderstanding of my teachings, which will inhibit humanity's spiritual evolution for nearly two millennia."

Then he added, "That's why I agreed to do this Gospel of the Second Coming and clear things up once and for all."

CHAPTER 2

The conversation really wasn't going as well as Jesus had hoped. He was starting to regret ever letting himself be talked into a comeback. He'd been perfectly content hanging out in eternity and wasn't interested in a sequel. After all, what could match the success of his last appearance? But that was all before he read that damn book.

Freke and Gandy had sent him a copy of their latest publication, *The Laughing Jesus,* probably hoping for a review. Eternity is a long time and there's nothing much to do, so the Lord actually read it—and boy, he learned a thing or two!

He had been very taken with the title, which made him feel that it was time to lighten up. So he had gone straight out and borrowed Freke and Gandy's other books from the Akashic Library, put his feet up, and with a cup of cocoa, indulged his rather narcissistic hobby of reading books about himself.

In *The Jesus Mysteries,* Freke and Gandy claim that Jesus is a mythical figure, not a historical man. *Explosive stuff!* Then they followed this up with *Jesus and the Lost Goddess,* in which they showed that Christianity originally involved a Goddess. *Bombshell!!* And they topped that off in *The Laughing Jesus,* with a blistering assault on the pernicious power of organized religion. *Ker-POW!!!*

What impressed the Lord most about these rather controversial books was the meticulous research and the way everything was backed up with copious footnotes—not that he read them, because he was a "big picture" sort of guy and didn't want to get bogged down in the details. It just made him assume the authors must know what they were talking about.

Freke and Gandy's theories didn't come as a complete surprise to the Lord, who had realized that he didn't really exist as soon as he had died and resurrected. But in these books he found the proof, both historical and philosophical, to back up his intuition. It was a revelation.

In fact, the Lord couldn't help hoping that Freke and Gandy were working on a fourth installment of their Jesus trilogy, and that's what made him spontaneously decide to contact them.

It was an unthought-out, spur-of-the-moment type thing, typical of people who live in the eternal now. He just wanted to tell them, from personal experience, that they'd sell a ton more books if they put their ideas across in a work of fiction.

Freke and Gandy had been hoping to hear from Jesus, because he was central to their latest half-baked scheme to change the world. They told him they'd already had the idea about writing fiction and suggested getting together for a chat.

Jesus was keen on brainstorming creative ideas, but Freke and Gandy clearly had their own agenda right from the start. They were adamant that the way forward was to write a new, more entertaining version of the Jesus story, and they wanted the Lord to reprise his starring role. They had even come up with a catchy title: *The Gospel of the Second Coming.*

To be honest, they originally wanted to write Jesus out of the story altogether, because he caused so many problems. But that wasn't so easy since the original Jesus story had been like the pilot for a soap opera that now had people really hooked.

So they came to the conclusion that the only thing to do was to make up a new story about Jesus in which he repeated all the nice things he said before about love and forgiveness, but without any of the nasty bits about eternal damnation and gnashing of teeth. Then, perhaps, it would be easier to write Jesus out altogether.

At first the Lord wasn't taken with the idea, because he felt that Freke and Gandy were trying to bandwagon on his celebrity. For their part, Freke and Gandy reminded him that he had promised to make a final appearance at the End of Time, so maybe he could combine the two?

They went on to point out how successful *The Da Vinci Code* had been, showing that the public was ready for a new take on Christianity. On top of which they were confident that they could cajole some professor to write an Introduction to the book, so the project would have academic respectability. And if no one would put their career on the line like that, they'd just make someone up—no problem.

When that didn't cut it with the Lord, Freke and Gandy started to whine about having droned on for years about Jesus not really existing, but with very limited success. Perhaps if Jesus told them himself, people would finally listen? After all, he still had a modicum of authority, except among thinking people—and they weren't the problem.

Freke and Gandy were keen that this time there would be a lot more gags, which had to be a good thing, but the Lord was concerned about pushing the blasphemy boat because it was pointless to deliberately alienate people. But Freke and Gandy maintained that people without a sense of humor just weren't worth talking to anyway.

The Lord couldn't argue with that. So he started to warm to these two kooky guys and suggested changing the title to *The Gospel of the Laughing Jesus*. But, of course, they used that title last time.

What really swung it with the Lord was when Freke and Gandy started to guilt-trip him on how things had gone horribly wrong with Christianity. They went into the gory details about how religiously inspired conflicts were inexorably leading to Armageddon, and they told him about a bunch of fundamentalist Muslims, whom he didn't like the sound of one bit. And they mentioned something about how cool it would be if we could just get over this religion thing.

The Lord didn't say yes there and then; he just said he'd think about it. But as soon as he got home, he looked into all of the trouble spots of the world and found that Freke and Gandy were right: Religion *was* causing discord all over the place. And in many cases, he was horrified to discover that *he* was the problem.

So the Lord gave Freke and Gandy a call to tell them he was up for it, because he realized that this was his opportunity to save the world for real. And, anyway, he quite fancied getting back into the limelight. Then he dropped into the conversation that he was working up a few new parables already.

But Jesus ditched his own ideas as soon as he looked at Freke and Gandy's script. It was just so good that his stuff paled in comparison. It was theological dynamite. He liked the way it spoke to the ironic sensibilities of the postmodern world. It was multidimensional and offered him a part that he could really get his teeth into. It gave him a reason to get back in there and transform the Jesus story.

Jesus could see that a co-production with Freke and Gandy was a win-win situation: He wanted to help spread their ideas to a wider audience, and they wanted a commercial success so they could finally make some money. It was a marriage made in Heaven.

It was during rehearsals that artistic differences began to surface. The Lord argued that seeing as he'd made the mess in the first place, it was his job to clear things up in the new version of the Jesus story. But Freke and Gandy were of the opinion that only the reader could really sort out the problem. Jesus just had to accept that this time he couldn't do it for them—they had to do it for themselves.

The Lord was reluctant to go along with this because he could be a bit of a prima donna sometimes. But after much explanation, he really got into the idea that the only way was to save the world soul by soul . . . reader by reader.

Once they got him on track, Freke and Gandy persuaded Jesus that the best way to do this was to go back into his story and actually give the teachings of Gnosis for real, not just promise to explain everything later, like he did last time.

Freke and Gandy had this hypothesis that in Christian mythology, Mary represented the soul of the reader. So they suggested that it would be symbolically satisfying if, over the course of their new gospel, Jesus transformed Mary by telling her everything he'd been told by them.

It was a bold plan but worth a go. If they could seduce the reader into identifying with the transformation of Mary, the reader would be transformed by proxy. And then they'd be ready to save the world. Hooray!

The Lord wasn't sure about sharing top billing with anyone. But Freke and Gandy went on about how sexy Mary Magdalene was right now, especially with women, and they bought far more of these sorts of books than men. Plus the Goddess thing was big again. And Mary was associated with all that in the popular mind.

Jesus had a soft spot for Mary. She was a nice girl—big heart, great legs. According to the Gospel of Philip, "The Lord loved Mary more than the other disciples, and he kissed her often on her . . ." Anyway, that's personal stuff that mustn't get into the tabloids. The scandal might jeopardize the Second Coming.

Suffice it to say, the Lord agreed that saving Mary was his best bet. After all, there wasn't much chance of getting through to Peter. And the rest of the twelve were just extras. He was ashamed to admit that he couldn't remember most of their names because they changed so alarmingly from gospel to gospel.

So that was that. It was decided that transforming Mary would be the underlying narrative structure of the new-look Jesus story. And secretly the Lord hoped that if he could reach Mary, perhaps she would be able to reach Peter since they'd known each other for years. If only he could stop them from arguing all the time.

The Lord felt confident that Mary would be open to the Gnosis. She would like the idea that she was a character in a story, because she had always wanted to be an actress. Surely he was offering her a role that any woman would die for: the tart with a heart who saves humanity?! And he knew that, deep down, Mary really wanted to save the world—whereas Peter just wanted to save for his holidays.

But the Lord was nervous about strutting his stuff again. Had he lost his touch? Could he really tell Mary all that he learned since he died and resurrected? How would he reveal to her that she existed in a story being imagined by the Author?

He really wanted Mary to experience Gnosis for herself. Then she'd realize how much better everything gets once you know that you don't really exist. That was his priority. But Mary had a "follower of the living master" thing going that made it practically impossible. So he decided that before he could go into the deep stuff, he'd have to get Mary to stop taking him literally.

Freke and Gandy suggested that the best way to start was by examining the evidence that proved Jesus wasn't a historical person.

Once that was out of the way, the Lord could go on to make the secrets of Gnosis really accessible by explaining all the spiritual jargon he used last time. Then he'd be in a position to explain the true allegorical meaning of the Jesus myth, which would really blow everyone's mind.

Jesus said he liked all that, but he was very excited by his own idea. As the climax of the whole gospel, he could give Mary a vision of the End of Time, because it's one of those things you just can't imagine until you experience it for yourself. Plus, he'd have kept his promise about coming back for the Last Judgment, which would be a real weight off his mind. So Freke and Gandy said they'd write in this finale as long as it was funny and played well with the focus groups.

Then they warned Jesus not to lose the plot. It was no good coming straight in trying to tell everyone that they were just characters in a story. They'd been there, done that. But of course the Lord couldn't resist giving it a go, although he regretted being so pigheaded now. After the mess he'd made of Chapter 1, he was beginning to wonder why he'd ever let himself be co-opted into such a harebrained project.

Anyway I'm just the narrator, and I've been going on for too long. I just wanted to fill you in on some of the background because this gospel is going to be pretty trip-hop, and you'll need all the orientation you can get. I don't want to say too much because it will preempt the story, but I can promise you one Hell of a roller-coaster ride through history, philosophy, and mythology . . . spiced with a healthy smattering of parody.

We join the Lord again as he is thinking about Freke and Gandy. And what a downer it was that he'd ever met those guys.

CHAPTER 3

"Okay. Let's try this again," said the Lord. Then putting on his "this is a test question" voice, he demanded of the disciples, "Who do you say I am?"

Peter was first with his hand up, because he knew the answer to this one saying, "Master, I say you are the Christ."

"Okay. But do you know what that means?"

"Not really. Something to do with that prophecy about Joshua coming again to whip the butt of those Roman bastards who are oppressing us?"

Then Mary interrupted, showing off the new, assertive style she'd acquired since she'd been hanging out with the Son of God, saying, "Be silent, Peter. You're a disgraceful example of a man who hasn't discovered his feminine side. Jesus isn't that clichéd all-action superhero type of messiah. He's a new, sensitive, caring type of Chosen One."

"Don't give me all that trendy bleeding-heart liberal hogwash!" replied Peter, who was used to Mary butting in with smart-arse comments, because she was always trying to get Jesus's attention.

"Watch it, big boy," retorted Mary. "Your testosterone levels are out of control again."

"Enough already!" said Jesus and he raised his eyes to Heaven to offer a prayer to the Author, saying, "Grant me patience with these two!"

There was an awkward silence while everyone paused to see if the Author would or wouldn't grant Jesus patience. Then Peter got fed up waiting, so he demanded, "Just tell us who you are, for Heaven's sake!"

And the Lord explained, "Well, there are a lot of theories to choose from. Some say I am a militant rabbi, a Jewish Zealot, or a mystical Essene. Others say I am a wandering Cynic philosopher, a magician, or a shaman. The Hindus claim that I am an incarnation of Vishnu, and a growing number of people imagine that I once visited India. Lots of folk have a vague picture of me as some sort of enlightened Buddha-figure . . . especially the Buddhists.

"Then there's the fruitier end of things. Erich von Däniken claims I'm a spaceman. Dan Brown has made a pile out of his theory, or should I say someone else's theory: that I'm the father of a line of European aristocrats. And John Allegro thinks that I'm a magic mushroom."

"That would certainly explain why this conversation seems so trippy!" interjected Mary.

And the Lord continued, "You would have thought that the sheer number of Jesuses constructed out of the so-called evidence might have alerted people to just how ambivalent and contradictory that evidence really is. But I guess people believe what they want to believe."

"This is all very confusing," commented Mary. "Maybe the time has come to clear things up, Lord? Who do you think is right?"

"In my opinion, Freke and Gandy are nearest to the truth," enthused Jesus, pleased that he had managed to steer the conversation so skillfully in the right direction.

Then, worried that he was in danger of coming across as a mere mouthpiece for Freke and Gandy, he added condescendingly, "Although their writing style can be irritatingly full of ironic self-references, an awful amount of annoying alliteration—and they use too many exclamation marks!!!

"In terms of scholarship they are pygmies standing on the shoulders of giants. Nonetheless, they have done a remarkable job in synthesizing the discoveries of others into a coherent and compelling thesis. To the bouquet of other's thoughts they have added the ribbon."

"That is so poetic," said Mary, realizing what it was about Jesus that made her tingle inside.

"I know nothing of this Freke and Gandy of whom you speak," complained Peter.

"Do not feel ashamed, Peter, because a surprising number of people haven't yet come across their groundbreaking work," consoled Jesus. "Freke and Gandy have been lacerating themselves on the cutting edge of scholarship for years now, but they still haven't received the large royalty checks they deserve. You should check out *The Jesus Mysteries* and their other books; they're very persuasive. Don't let all the footnotes put you off, because they're a rollicking good read."

So Peter asked, "What do Freke and Gandy claim? Can you put it in a nutshell for me? Because they don't sound like my sort of books—and anyway, I can't read."

And the Lord explained, "Their basic point is that there never was a historical Jesus. They say that the Jesus story is a Jewish reworking of various Pagan myths of a dying and resurrecting Son of God who is both God and man. These myths were everywhere in the ancient world. Here's a list of astonishing similarities between the Jesus story and the Pagan myths, which Freke and Gandy always put in their books somewhere:

- The mother of the Pagan Godman is a mortal virgin and his father is God.

- He is born in a cave or humble cowshed on December 25 in front of shepherds.

- He surrounds himself with twelve disciples.

- He offers his followers the chance to be born again through the rites of baptism.

- He miraculously turns water into wine at a marriage ceremony.

- He rides triumphantly into town on a donkey while people wave palm leaves to honor him.

- He attacks the religious authorities, who set out to destroy him.

- He dies at Easter time as a sacrifice for the sins of the world, sometimes through crucifixion.

- On the third day he rises from the dead and ascends to Heaven in glory.

- His followers await his return as the judge during the Last Days.

- His death and resurrection are celebrated by a ritual meal of bread and wine that symbolize his body and blood.

- By symbolically sharing in his death and resurrection, his followers believe they will also share in his spiritual resurrection and know eternal life."

"So everything you did was ripped off from the Pagans!" exclaimed Mary, feeling cheated.

"That's a little harsh," said Jesus, looking genuinely upset. "I prefer to think that my story contains many clever literary allusions."

Mary continued thoughtfully, "Now I stop and think about it, the Jesus story is clearly mythological. I mean, does the virgin birth really sound likely, when we all know it takes two to tango?"

"It's not meant to be taken *seriously,*" explained the Lord. "After all, if the Magi had really turned up with all that gold, do you think Mary and Joseph would have left me in that manger with the donkeys? No, sir—they'd have been checking into the nearest Holiday Inn faster than you can say hallelujah!"

"And what about the star that announced your birth?" added Mary. "I've never seen a star travel through the sky and come to rest over a single building!"

"It's crazy," agreed Jesus, "and clearly a fire hazard."

Then Peter suggested, "Perhaps some of the Jesus story is a bit far-fetched, but couldn't there be a kernel of truth to it?"

And the Lord replied, "All that really matters is this: Did I really die and resurrect? Because that's the foundation of Christian theology. Once you realize that *all* the Godmen of the ancient world died and resurrected, that foundation collapses and the whole edifice comes crumbling down."

But Peter objected, "Just because a lot of Pagan stuff has gotten into the Jesus story doesn't necessarily mean that we never existed historically. I like the idea of us being basically real, albeit with some mythological overlays."

"That is the usual response people have when first confronted with the evidence," replied Jesus. "But the trouble is, when you strip out all of the mythic elements from the Jesus story, there's nothing left. So what can be said about the man who is supposedly buried beneath all the myths? Nothing!"

"But you *must* exist, because you started Christianity," insisted Peter, now getting impatient with all this nonsense. "Religions don't begin all by themselves—you have to have a founder."

"Not true," replied Jesus. "The cult of the Pagan Godman Mithras spread from Persia to Portugal to Spain and even to Scotland, yet there never was a Mithras. Lots of religions have been very successful despite not having a historical founder. I mean, do you think Krishna, Ram, and all those Hindu guys are for real?"

Then he added, "In the last UK census, a third of a million people put their religion as 'Jedi Knight.' Give it another couple of centuries and they'll be arguing about the historical existence of Obi-Wan Kenobi!"

CHAPTER 4

"**I** can't believe that Jews would adopt Pagan mythology," protested Peter. "The Pagans are really dumb and worship lots of gods with animal heads, whereas we Jews are really smart."

"Actually, that's all bunk and merely shows that you've been hanging out in the land of fiction for too long," replied Jesus. "The Pagan world is very sophisticated, whereas we Jews hardly had any culture to speak of before we were conquered by the Greeks three centuries before I wasn't really born. Since then we've become extremely Hellenized."

But Peter wasn't having any of it, so he continued, "The Pagans may love their silly mythological fantasies, but we Jews do history."

"The thing is, Peter," explained Jesus, "everything you take to be history is really mythology. All those stories of Adam and Eve, the Flood, the Exodus, Moses and the Promised Land, David and Goliath— none of it actually happened. You should check out scholars such as Thomas Thompson and Israel Finkelstein. They've done a fantastic job demolishing the historicity of the Old Testament. And these guys are professors! And some of them are Jewish!"

"That pretty much undermines traditional Judaism then," commented Mary.

"And it pretty much undermines Christianity, too," added the Lord.

"Because if there was no Adam and Eve, then there was no 'original sin.' Adam is obviously a mythical figure, so you don't need a historical savior to redeem the original sin of the mythical Adam. The whole thing stands or falls together."

"So," said Mary, "the Jesus story is just another example of Jewish mythmaking?"

"Exactly," commended the Lord. "I am a synthesis of the Pagan Godman with Joshua, the mythical Messiah of the Old Testament. 'Jesus' is the Greek translation of the name 'Joshua.' It's a sign of how Greek I am that you guys keep calling me 'Jesus' instead of 'Joshua'!"

"Did you hear that, boys?" shouted Peter excitedly to the disciples, who had been passing the time playing backgammon in the background. "Jesus is Joshua come again!"

"Don't get us involved. We never say or do anything much," piped up one of the disciples.

"You're right—you're just walk-on parts," agreed Jesus. "All that is important is that I collect twelve disciples around me, because that's what Joshua did. They represent the twelve tribes of Israel if you're Jewish or the twelve signs of the zodiac if you're Pagan. A nice bit of syncretism, even if I say so myself."

"So the whole Jesus thing is just a story," concluded Mary, starting to really get it.

"Not *just* a story," corrected Jesus. "It's the greatest story ever told. And one of the oldest. It originated in Egypt as the myth of Osiris; the Greeks transformed it into the myth of Dionysus; and in the hands of the Persians, it became the myth of Mithras. In fact, every culture around the Mediterranean created its own version of the cult of the dying and resurrecting Godman. So it's no surprise that the Jews did the same."

"But if there wasn't a historical Jesus born in the year zero, when did Christianity really begin?" asked Mary, hoping to impress the Lord with her inquiring mind.

And Jesus answered: "Hellenized Jews had been synthesizing the Pagan mysteries with their own Jewish mysteries of Moses and Joshua for centuries, so the prototype Jesus story was created way before my supposed birth. According to Freke and Gandy, I was dreamed up by Jews in Alexandria, which was a multicultural melting pot—the New York City of the ancient world. A quarter of the population were Jews, who spoke Greek and were educated in Greek philosophy. They wrote lots of works that combined Jewish and Pagan mythology, and they were all written in Greek like the gospels. The Jesus story is just another example of this literary genre."

"So who created the Jesus myth?" inquired Mary, feeling she was coming across as quite the intellectual.

"Lots of people played a part," explained Jesus. "It started as a very basic allegory about spiritual death and resurrection, but over the years many different authors added more and more elements from Jewish and Pagan mythology until we got the full-blown Jesus story we all know and love."

"But why did Jews want to merge Judaism with Pagan mythology?" asked Mary, trying to ask all the right questions.

And the Lord replied: "Greek culture was the American culture of the ancient world: Everyone loved to hate it, but they all wanted a slice because it was so damn good! Traditional Judaism was too primitive in comparison—too many petty rules and regulations, not to mention the necessity for men to have their foreskins chopped off! Hellenized Jews knew they needed a new religion that was less exclusive and more integrated with the dominant culture of the day. Many of them had been initiated into the Pagan mystery religions, and they wanted to temper Judaism with the more enlightened thinking of the Greek philosophers. So they decided to transform the genocidal Joshua of Judaism into the gentle Jesus of Christianity."

"I get it!" enthused Mary. "That's why you're a completely different kind of Joshua from the bloodthirsty bastard who ethnically cleansed Canaan on Jehovah's orders. Traditional Jews expect you to go about whipping up a Jewish army to defeat the Romans, but instead, you're the prince of peace."

"These Hellenized Jews are feta-eating surrender monkeys," complained Peter belligerently. "We don't want a Messiah who will philosophize the Romans out of existence. We want someone to give them a good kicking!"

"That's precisely the attitude the Hellenized Jews were trying to counter," explained Jesus. "You see, religious fanaticism had really taken off among traditional Jews, and the Hellenized Jews could see that it was inspiring a bellicose nationalism that would eventually drive the Romans to destroy the state of Israel altogether."

"That'll never happen," asserted Peter confidently.

"Unfortunately, it's exactly what *is* going to happen," contradicted the Lord.

And Peter cried out in anguish, "A prophecy of doom!!!"

"Yes," conceded Jesus. "But, like all of my prophecies, it's pronounced after the event."

Then, keen to show how much she understood, Mary concluded, "So Jesus is a literary critique of Joshua, created by Hellenized Jews to replace traditional Jewish religion with something a bit more Greek."

"Exactly," commended Jesus. "And in this Gospel of the Second Coming, I've been transformed into a new Jesus who combines ancient mythology with Anglo-American culture in an attempt to replace traditional Christianity with something a lot more fun and funky for the twenty-first century."

CHAPTER 5

"What are the earliest texts written by Hellenized Jews that are specifically Christian?" asked Mary, sounding as though she was working on a Ph.D. in religious studies.

"Those would be Shorty's letters, written in the early first century," replied Jesus.

Then he added, "Actually he's a bit touchy about being vertically challenged, so most people call him 'Paul,' which means 'Shorty' but doesn't sound as rude."

"Who's this geezer, Paul? I've never heard of him," grumbled Peter.

So the Lord explained, "Paul comes from Tarsus, which is almost as cosmopolitan a city as Alexandria. He's a Hellenized Jew who hopes that by combining the myths of Joshua and the Greek Godman into the Jesus myth, he can break down the barriers that divide the Jews and Gentiles. But his version of the Jesus story is very early, so it's pretty sketchy compared with the blockbuster we get later."

Then the Lord grimaced and added, "Unfortunately, Paul's had bad press. If you read the letters attributed to him in the New Testament, he'd give you the creeps. All that stuff about women sitting at the back and keeping their mouths shut. Slavery is okay, but being queer is a no-no. He comes across as a weird, sexist homophobe."

Mary looked horrified, so Jesus reassured her, saying, "Relax, Mary. Paul didn't write any of that stuff. Only half of the letters attributed to him in the New Testament are really by Paul—the rest are forgeries. You should read *The Gnostic Paul* by Elaine Pagels; the evidence is all in there. That woman is one smart cookie!"

Then, with obvious fondness, he added, "Ah, Paul! Part Jew, part Greek, part Danny DeVito. He's all things to all men—a bit like me. Would you care to meet him?"

And so it came to pass that Jesus raised his hands (to show he had nothing up his sleeves) and theatrically pronounced, "Hocussss . . . pocusssss. . . ." Whereupon a short, balding man, the spitting image of Danny DeVito, miraculously materialized.

As the whistles and applause from the disciples died down, the Lord spoke to the disoriented figure, saying, "Hello. I'm Jesus."

"Come again?" replied Paul.

"Do you mean 'pardon' or do you mean 'come again'?" asked Jesus politely.

"I mean, who in God's name are you?" explained Paul.

And the Lord suggested, "Think of me as a literary embodiment of your 'Christ within.'"

Paul looked dubious, so Jesus continued, "I thought it was about time we had a chat. Mary has a lot of questions for you."

Mary offered her hand to Paul, who held on to it for longer than was strictly necessary. Then he drawled, "Dinnngg donnnggg! Why haven't we met before?"

"It's probably because I'm a character in an allegorical gospel," explained Mary, blushing. "I've only just found out."

"So you're an actress," purred Paul. "How exciting!"

"And you're a great writer, I hear," replied Mary, feeling a bit flustered.

"I was just telling Mary about your famous letters," explained Jesus. "I'm interested to hear your reactions to the New Testament. It's been a huge international bestseller. Do you feel it lives up to all the hype?"

Paul didn't know what to say. He had only recently found out that he was a published author, whilst waiting for his cue in the green-room backstage, when someone had suggested he should really take a quick look through the New Testament, as Jesus was sure to ask for his opinion about it.

He had to admit it was a bit of an ego rush to see some of his letters in print, because, to be honest, at the time they were only read by a small handful of mystics and misfits. He was horrified, however, to see a whole lot of other letters claiming to be from him, but they were written by some other Paul, who was clearly not a very nice piece of work.

He'd quite enjoyed the story about Jesus at the beginning of the book, but it was plainly plagiarized, and he could have done without the three subsequent repeats, because once you knew the ending it ruined the dramatic tension.

The truth was he couldn't stand the book. It was confusing, contradictory, and badly edited. The only really good thing about the New Testament was the idea that it consigned the Old Testament to the compost heap of history, because that truly was unmitigated crap, as he'd said before in his Letter to the Philippians.

But the problem for Paul was that he really hated being negative, because deep down he wanted everyone to like him, so he desperately searched for something positive to say. Eventually he came up with: "It's got a commercial title. People like new versions of old things."

Then he added, "And it's certainly a novel idea to set the myth of the dying and resurrecting Godman in Jerusalem. Is it the script for a new mystery play?"

"It's claimed to be a historical account of Jesus's once-only visit to planet Earth," explained the Lord. "The same Jesus you met on the road to Damascus."

"What absolute nonsense!" exclaimed Paul unable to control himself. "I never met a historical Jesus; I experienced a vision of light. In my Letter to the Galatians, I clearly state that everything I know about Jesus came to me through revelation. My letters don't mention any details about Jesus's life, except that he died and resurrected, which is an allegory for spiritual rebirth."

"But surely you must quote some of Jesus's words?" insisted Mary.

"What words? My Christ is a version of the old Pagan idea of the *Logos,* which represents the divinity within all of us. As I said in my Letter to the Colossians, the 'Great Secret' stored up since the foundation of the world is that Christ is within you. If the Great Secret were that Christ had been born down the road in a shed, don't you think I would have said so?!"

Then he added, "It sounds as though my new take on the Joshua story has gotten horrendously out of hand. Maybe I'd better go and write some more letters to clear things up?"

"I'm sorry to say that if you wrote any new letters, most Christians wouldn't bother to read them," cautioned the Lord. "Several texts ascribed to Paul were found among the Gnostic manuscripts at Nag Hammadi, but hardly any Christians have given them a cursory glance. They're very closed-minded like that."

"How about if I beef up the stuff about not falling back from a spiritual understanding of Jesus into a mere worldly understanding?" offered Paul, itching to get that quill in his hand. "I could add a warning about people who preach 'another Jesus.' Do you think that will help?"

"You said *all* that last time and it did no good," replied Jesus, keen to discourage Paul from writing any more mystical letters—the last lot had caused enough confusion.

Then he took Paul by the hand and said, "Anyway, you've been very helpful, but we must crack on. It has been a pleasure to meet you at last."

"The pleasure has been all mine," replied Paul affectionately. "It's been most enlightening. I feel as if before I met you face-to-face, I was only seeing things through a glass darkly."

And turning to Mary, Paul bid her farewell, saying, "If you're ever at a loose end, darling, maybe we could set up our own cult together. How do you fancy the role of my intoxicated prophetess?"

"I've really enjoyed our brief encounter," cooed Mary, stooping down to give Paul a little peck on the cheek, whereupon he disappeared in an unexpected vision of radiant light.

"What a charmer," gushed Mary.

"Smarmy midget," muttered Peter under his breath.

"He certainly is charismatic," agreed Jesus, "but I think I should warn you that according to early Christian tradition, Paul already has an ongoing relationship with an intoxicated priestess. She's a lovely lass called Thecla, and he travels around with her, preaching his mysteries of Jesus. . . . So don't get your hopes up."

CHAPTER 6

""How ow did a cuddly mystic like Paul ever get transformed into the authoritarian bigot of the New Testament?" asked Mary.

"He got caught up in a civil war within the Christian community," explained Jesus.

"At last some action!" exclaimed Peter with relief. "This I want to hear!"

So the Lord continued, "The conflict was between two different types of Christians. On the one side there were the original Christians, such as Paul, who knew that the Jesus story was an allegorical myth encoding the secrets of Gnosis. And on the other side, there were those who had come to believe that it *literally* happened. Let's call them 'Gnostics' and 'Literalists.'"

"I'm going to support the Literalists," declared Peter, "because we've just met a Gnostic and he was a smug git!"

"Well, I like the sound of the Gnostics because I thought Paul was a sweetheart," retorted Mary. "Who do you support, Lord?"

"I'm not interested in taking sides; I just want you to know the truth," said Jesus, which wasn't entirely honest because really he was rooting for the Gnostics, too.

Then he added, "The quickest way to discover the truth is for you to meet one of the greatest liars of all time—the man who really got the whole Literalist bandwagon rolling in the second century. And, unlike Paul, he really is a weird, sexist homophobe."

Whereupon Jesus waved his hands wildly over his head and intoned the magic words: "Izzy, wizzy, let's get busy."

Suddenly a devious-looking man who bore a striking resemblance to L. Ron Hubbard appeared before them. It was basically the same trick as before, so there was less applause this time.

Jesus welcomed the stranger, saying, "Sorry to bother you, Bishop Irenaeus, but I'm interested in understanding how one goes about setting up a religious cult, and I regard you as the main man in this area."

Bishop Irenaeus really didn't have time for all this because he had a business to run. But on the other hand, he was always eager to give advice whether people wanted it or not—especially when it meant he could talk about himself.

He began by explaining authoritatively, "The secret to thriving in the cult industry is simple: Give the customers what they want. That's all I did and look at me today—I'm a bishop. From 'nobodi-ness' to 'your holiness' in a few short years."

"I'm impressed already," whispered Peter, nudging Mary in the ribs.

And Irenaeus continued, "The key is to have a clear brand image. It's the only way to stand out in the crowded spiritual marketplace. For example, I've built up a nice little business using an utterly innovative marketing angle: I offer people a new take on an old story. I make the audacious claim that the myth of the dying and resurrecting Pagan Godman has actually been *lived out* by my God-man Jesus."

"You need a great gimmick like that to get the attention of the buying public," agreed Peter.

"But then you need to follow through by offering a product people want at very little cost," cautioned Irenaeus. "So I offer my customers an attractive deal. All they have to do is believe that the Jesus story really happened, and they'll be off to paradise when they kick the bucket. Then, once they're hooked, I slip in that they're also expected to tithe 10 percent of their income to my church!"

"I like the way you think," acknowledged Peter respectfully.

"It's been a hugely successful promotional campaign," boasted Irenaeus. "Everyone loved it—except the Gnostics, of course, who started spreading it around that I was running an 'imitation church.'"

"That's fair enough," interrupted Mary. "After all, the Gnostics invented Christianity. You just turned it into a business."

But Irenaeus ignored her because he never paid attention to women, as they had nothing sensible to say.

So he went on venomously: "God, I hate those Gnostic faggots. They're all bloody heretics and homos. They undermined my whole sales strategy by telling my recruits that the Jesus story was a giant allegory, and they could explain what it meant. And they just wouldn't stop repeating their slogan 'Jesus didn't come in the flesh.'

"I was determined to stop those agenda-benders queering my pitch. I needed authoritative texts that I could claim to be eyewitness accounts of Jesus's life. That would show those buggers. Texts were weapons in my struggle with the Gnostics, and I wanted a big black book in my arsenal, like the Old Testament—only newer, the New Testament.

"But I had a problem. The world was awash with hundreds of different Christian gospels in which Jesus was clearly mythological. So I put together four gospels that made Jesus sound like a real person, and I attributed them to Matthew, Mark, Luke, and John. Then, in a bold bit of aggressive marketing, I told the world that only these gospels were 'orthodox' and all the others were 'heretical.' I was the first to coin the terms!"

"You're an inspiration!" beamed Peter.

"Of course I knew people would complain that my gospels were written far too late to really be eyewitness accounts, but I figured it was perfectly possible that some of Jesus's disciples had lived into their 80s, learned Greek, and retired to write their memoirs. That neatly explained all of the contradictions between the gospels, because venerable elders are prone to the odd 'senior moment' and get easily confused."

"So you actually had some personal reminiscences about Jesus's life!" enthused Peter, pleased to find definitive proof that the Lord must be wrong about not really existing.

"Who cares? Probably not. The writers of the gospels of Matthew and Luke have clearly borrowed text from the Gospel of Mark, sometimes word for word. And the geography in Mark is all over the place, so whoever wrote it obviously had never been to Palestine. But none of my flock was sophisticated enough to notice any of that.

"I had more of a problem with the fourth gospel in my little collection, which was originally called the Gospel of the Beloved Disciple. The Gnostics insisted that the Beloved Disciple was Mary Magdalene, but I knew I would never sell a gospel written by a woman to my misogynist Roman client base. Then I had a brain wave. I realized that with a few little tweaks to the text, I could turn the Beloved Disciple into a man and repackage the work as the Gospel of John."

"God, you're good!" declared Peter in awe.

"So now I had four gospels that proved the historical existence of Jesus—all written by men. Of course, those Gnostic lady-boys didn't like that because they treated women as equals."

"That's scandalous!" exclaimed Peter.

"Mind you, we had to make some changes to the Jesus story along the way. To stop the Pagans claiming we ripped off their ancient mythology, we bolstered the impression that Jesus was a real person by weaving some genuine historical figures into the story, such as John the Baptist and Pontius Pilate. Unfortunately, we got some of the details wrong, like calling Pilate a procurator when he was actually a prefect, but anyone who wasn't there could have made a mistake like that."

"Fair enough," interjected Peter sympathetically.

"I still had to deal with the problem that it was the Romans who killed Jesus, which wouldn't go down well in my manor. So with various rewrites over the years, we shifted the responsibility to the Jews. Finally, we put the words *Let his blood be on us and on our children!* into the mouth of the Jews, while portraying a Roman centurion as the only one to realize that Jesus truly was the Son of God."

"Job done!" announced Peter, who was so in awe of Irenaeus's creative talents that he was thinking of dropping his Jewish affiliations and becoming a Roman.

"Now I had to deal with the problem of Paul. He was the 'Great Apostle' of the Gnostics, who they claimed got the whole Christian thing going in the first place. He was just too well known to be ignored. So I came up with a cunning plan."

"I just knew you would!" squeaked Peter in delight.

And Irenaeus leaned toward him and whispered conspiratorially, "First I produced an original text called the Acts of the Apostles that makes it clear that Paul isn't a real apostle at all since he didn't actually meet Jesus. Then I made up a few extra letters from Paul in which he venomously lambastes the Gnostics, puts down women, says that slavery is okay, and most important, attacks poofters . . . the kind of thing that any sober right-minded Roman citizen would agree with."

"Well said!" interjected Peter, who had never been quite this impressed by anyone. It made him wonder what he'd ever seen in Jesus.

"That's when I had another stroke of genius: To make sure that no one noticed that Paul's Jesus was clearly mythic, I put all his letters *after* the gospels in the New Testament, even though they were actually written much earlier. So now when readers come to Paul, they naturally assume that he must be talking about the Jesus of the gospels."

"That's *so* clever!" pronounced Peter in astonishment.

Then Irenaeus declared triumphantly, "And while I was on a creative roll, I made up some letters by John and Peter that warned that anyone who denied that Jesus really came 'in the flesh' was a heretic."

"It's exactly the kind of thing I would have written, if only I could write," acknowledged Peter.

And sounding very pleased with himself, Irenaeus added, "Finally, to wind it all up, I rewrote a Jewish apocalyptic text called Revelation as a Christian nightmare designed to scare the pants off everybody."

"You can't make religion work without fear," agreed Peter enthusiastically.

"Throw the whole lot together and presto! Literalist Christianity not only had a new historical angle on the old Pagan Godman story, but we had a big book to back it up. Now I was ready to teach those Gnostic cocksuckers a thing or two about setting up a multinational cult."

"Go for it!" shouted Peter, punching the air.

"It was easy because the Gnostic sales pitch was amateur crap. They told people not to follow anyone and to become a Christ themselves, but any fool can see that most people don't have the time to become a Christ. The Gnostics insisted that God was ineffable, but it's obvious that the common man wants statues and a holy book to kiss. The Gnostics encouraged everyone to think for themselves, but the fact is, Joe Public prefers to go along with the herd."

"It's always safer with the herd," interjected Peter.

"So I offered an off-the-shelf religion, in which thinking for yourself was not only unnecessary, it was positively discouraged because I had all the answers in the Bible. And this left my grateful followers free to go about their daily business, safe in the knowledge that someone somewhere knew what was going on. All they had to do was have faith . . . or at least say they did once a week."

"No one ever got poor underestimating the intelligence of the *populus Romani*," said Peter, because he heard someone say something like that once, and it sounded like a cool thing to say.

"Those Gnostic nancy boys just don't get it. If you want to move ideas from the margin to the mainstream, you have to accept that they will inevitably get diluted. People want a real-life superhero, not allegorical myths. I guess you could say that if the historical Jesus hadn't existed, we would've had to invent him—"

"Which is exactly what you did!" interrupted Mary, who was so furious she could hardly resist the temptation to lay one on the contemptible shyster.

And she probably would have, but Irenaeus suddenly remembered that he had a business to run, and hurriedly concluded, "So that's how it's done. If you're looking for a consultant to help you set up your new cult, my rates are very reasonable as long as you don't read the small print."

"I'm not really into organized religion," said Jesus, relieved that the despicable old windbag had finally stopped. "I just wanted your input for this Gospel of the Second Coming we're doing."

"Is it heretical?" asked Irenaeus suspiciously.

"Jesus! Make him shut up!" begged Mary. "I've heard enough!"

"Excellent," said Jesus, feeling Freke and Gandy would be pleased with the progress that Mary was making. Then he clapped his hands and Irenaeus disappeared in a green cloud of bile, yelling something offensive about "bloody Gnostic pillow biters," and that he would definitely be adding this new gospel to his blacklist as soon as he got home.

"A true visionary!" announced Peter, who felt that he now had all the information he needed to make it big-time in the religion racket.

And the Lord said sadly, "Irenaeus wrote five turgid volumes attacking the Gnostics, but he showed little interest in love, forgiveness, or any of the other great Christian values."

"But you've got to admire his ingenuity," insisted Peter. "He's the master of misinformation."

And the Lord agreed, saying, "Freke and Gandy accuse the Literalists of running a veritable fantasy factory, turning out endless forgeries to serve their ideological agenda."

Then he added sardonically, "But after this Gospel of the Second Coming, they may feel a little hypocritical."

Mary didn't hear any of that, however, because something Irenaeus had said was bothering her. So she asked the Lord, "Is it true that there will be a Gospel of John that's really written by me?"

"It's not actually written by you, Mary," replied the Lord, hoping not to disappoint her. "You're a character in the story."

Then, for the reader's benefit, he added, "I suggest visiting **www. beloveddisciple.org**, where the whole sorry business of the misattribution of the Fourth Gospel of John is explored in great detail."

And that was when John chipped in, saying, "I don't want to be remembered as the guy lying on the Lord's breast at the Last Supper. That makes me look, well, dodgy."

"It certainly makes much more sense once you realize it should be Mary," agreed the Lord, hoping he wasn't coming across as homophobic.

"I can remember when Mary would lie across *my* lap," muttered Bartholomew wistfully in the background.

"I can remember when Mary would lap dance for *all* her clients," commented another of the twelve, to general amusement.

CHAPTER 7

"So who won the war between the horrid Literalists and the yummy Gnostics?" asked Mary, crossing her fingers that the Gnostics would win, although she really wasn't sure this would help.

"I want to know, too," insisted Peter, "because I've put money on the Literalists in a wager with Thomas."

"Well, let's find out what happened, shall we?" said the Lord. Then he wiggled his nose—just like Samantha in *Bewitched*—and a rather startled bishop, in full ceremonial regalia, appeared before them.

There was no applause this time because the disciples had seen it all before. Anyway, most of them had become so bored with the conversation that they'd started a game of strip poker with Martha and Salome and didn't notice.

On realizing that he was in the presence of the Lord, the bishop threw himself to his knees and started kissing Jesus's ankles, feet, and even the floor after Jesus managed to move out of the way.

"Please stop groveling," said Jesus, looking irritated. "I can't stand groveling."

"Who is this sycophant?" asked Mary.

"This is Bishop Eusebius," explained Jesus. "He is the spiritual advisor to Emperor Constantine, who adopted Christianity as the religion of the Roman Empire at the beginning of the fourth century. Between them they created the conditions for the triumph of Literalist Christianity over all its rivals."

"*Yesssss!*" yelled Peter, unable to resist a little victory dance.

"I was just doing my bit for your church, Jesus," said Eusebius proudly, as he struggled to his feet, brushing down his ceremonial robes and putting his hat on straight.

"Indeed," agreed Jesus. "And your 'bit' involved telling some of the biggest lies in history."

"I just did what was necessary," explained Eusebius obsequiously. "The empire had been on the point of collapse for years, and Constantine looked as though he might be the one to hold it together. His mother, a devoted Christian I cannot praise highly enough, thought that he might be able to use some help from us bishops. It was the chance we'd been waiting for to go mainstream.

"The marriage of church and state was between partners who shared two particularly admirable features in common: a dogmatic certainty about their God-given right to rule over others and a willingness to back that up with extreme force. The result was that the Roman Empire was able to rebrand itself as the 'Holy' Roman Empire."

"The name over the door changed, but business carried on as usual," interjected Jesus.

"There's a lot to be said for stability and continuity," muttered Peter, counting the money he won from Thomas.

"But why did the Romans adopt Christianity as their state religion?" asked Mary, annoyed that Peter was making it so very clear that his side had won. "Didn't the Romans have enough gods already?"

"Stealing other people's gods was a bad habit with the Romans," explained Eusebius. "It was a kind of divine kleptomania, but it also made astute political sense. When a foreign cult got big enough to threaten the status quo, the authorities simply co-opted it and pressed it into the service of the empire."

"You've got to admire the Romans," admitted Peter. "They know how to keep a firm grip on the reins of power."

And Eusebius continued: "Over the centuries, different emperors tried to keep the empire united by encouraging the worship of various dying and resurrecting Godmen, nearly all of them adopted from countries they had conquered. None of them were much good. So Constantine tried Christianity, which at least was something new. Plus, it was popular with the army because they saw Jesus as a working-class hero who grew up a carpenter but became a celebrity."

Then the Lord explained, "Constantine had to fight five other emperors to become all-powerful, and they all had their favorite gods, any of whom could have become the patron deity of the empire. So it's just an accident of history that Christianity came to dominate Europe."

"I prefer to think of it as the Will of the Almighty," suggested Eusebius, who was in the business of finding better ways of putting things.

"Did it ever occur to you that in the process of gaining the whole world, Christianity might lose its own soul?" asked Mary.

And Eusebius replied with a shrug, "That happened years earlier. By the time I was running the business, the Gnostics' spineless philosophy of love and forgiveness had already been turned into a robust religion based on fear and guilt. My contribution was to align the Literalist Church with the Roman state, thereby allowing us to wipe out our critics."

"That's right," agreed the Lord accusingly. "Everyone had to follow the party line as laid down by your employer, Constantine, for whom you wrote a biography, portraying him as a veritable saint. But I suppose if anyone was in need of creative help with their CV, it was Constantine, because he actually was a complete monster who had murdered most of his immediate family!"

"Keep your voice down," whispered Eusebius, looking around nervously. "The Emperor has spies everywhere."

"So what happened to the Gnostics?" asked Mary, fearing the worst.

And Eusebius explained, "Me and the governor had to crack down on heretics to unite Christianity into one Universal Church. You can only achieve unity through uniformity."

"What's wrong with unity in variety?" asked Mary.

"That's what the Gnostics kept saying, before we bashed in their heads and burned all their books," replied Eusebius.

"Sometimes you have to torture a few dissidents to instill discipline in the ranks," conceded Peter.

By now Mary was nearly in tears, so she exclaimed emotionally, "I don't understand why you Literalists have to force your religion down everybody's throat!"

So Eusebius explained, "The only way to avoid eternal damnation is to believe in the true version of Christianity. Therefore we all have a duty to do anything in our power to convert unbelievers and save their souls—and I mean *anything*. It's a powerful moral imperative to forcefully evangelize the one true faith."

Then, in mock admiration, Jesus declared, "And your contribution to the great work of imposing a religious monoculture on the ancient world was to write *The History of the Church,* which has been regarded as definitive ever since."

"My *magnum opus,*" beamed Eusebius. "We needed an official version of events so that everyone was singing from the same hymn sheet."

"Is there anything you'd like to tell us about your 'history' of Christianity?" asked the Lord in his "patient headmaster" voice. "You didn't make it up, did you?"

"Not *completely,*" protested Eusebius. "Most of it had already been made up by my illustrious predecessors. I just organized the material, added my own little touches, and then indulged my predilection for bashing the Gnostics and the Jews."

"Indeed, you seem to relish the suffering of the Jews at the hands of the Romans and claim that it's God's punishment for murdering me!" replied Jesus. "There is page after page reveling in all the gruesome details about the starving mothers reduced to eating their own dead children, the thousands of crucifixions, and the millions sold into slavery."

"Lousy Yids!" exclaimed Eusebius. "We had to get rid of them because once we started spreading it around that the Christians were now 'God's Chosen People,' the Jews were an inconvenient anachronism."

"Yet I see you have plenty of respect for the Jewish historian Josephus," continued Jesus, "but, of course, he was in the pay of the Romans."

"You see, I'm not a racist," protested Eusebius. "More of a dogmatic ideologue."

Then the Lord announced, "I'd particularly like to talk to you about the famous passage in Josephus, in which he seems to talk about me in glowing terms as the Messiah—the passage that is continually referred to as definitive proof of my historical existence. What I find puzzling is that the third-century Christian Origen tells us categorically that there is no mention of me anywhere in the works of Josephus. Yet this passage suddenly appears in a copy of Josephus in *your* library, and scholars have noted that the language bears an uncanny resemblance to your own literary style. Do you have any thoughts about that?"

"Okay, okay, I'll tell you the truth," announced Eusebius, wondering what it would be like to actually tell the truth about something. "It *was* me! I made up all that stuff myself! It's what anyone would have done in my position. You see, none of the Roman historians had mentioned Jesus, which was a big embarrassment. After all, his death was meant to be accompanied by earthquakes, a total eclipse, and people coming back from the dead. You'd have thought someone would have noticed. Three Roman historians did mention 'Christians,' but no one was doubting the existence of Christians. What I needed was independent verification that the gospels were historical fact. So I added a few words to Josephus."

Then, unable to resist a snigger, the Lord asked, "And did you also make up that letter you refer to that was supposedly written by me to the Prince of Edessa—whoever he may be! I hope that isn't another forgery, because I'm sure my signature would be worth a fortune on eBay."

"It's quite obvious, Bishop Eusebius, that you're a lying little weasel in the pay of a fascist state," announced Mary.

"That is completely obvious if you look at the evidence," agreed Jesus, "which is why eminent scholars such as Jacob Burckhardt condemn Eusebius as 'the first thoroughly dishonest and unfair historian of ancient times.'"

And Eusebius cried indignantly, "Critics can carp from the sidelines, but my *History of the Church* was a huge bestseller!"

"Only because all of the texts that presented a different version of Christianity were thrown on bonfires by your boss's storm troopers," pointed out Jesus.

And Mary put it bluntly, saying, "You're not a historian at all, are you, Eusebius? You're Constantine's spin doctor, and your so-called *History of the Church* is just propaganda."

Then Jesus added provocatively, "He's the Goebbels of the Holy Roman Empire!"

"Who's Goebbels?" asked Peter.

"He's the Eusebius of the Nazi Party," explained Jesus. "Goebbels and his cronies tried to implement the final solution to the Jewish problem. It's a long story and I don't have time to explain, because we can now move on, as Mary has clearly gotten the message."

"I'd like to hear more about this 'final solution,'" requested Eusebius enthusiastically.

"I'll tell you all about it when we meet at the End of Time," replied the Lord.

Then he called out, "Beam him up, Scotty!"

As the disoriented bishop began to vibrate and fade away, the Lord called after him vindictively, "Just so you know, your attempt to enforce unity was a complete failure because the church eventually splintered into over twenty thousand denominations. And that's a Hell of a lot of competing Christianities . . . especially if only one of them is right!"

CHAPTER 8

"**S**o there it is," declared the Lord, preparing to wrap up the first section of this gospel, which deals with history. "I started off as a mythical synthesis of the Pagan Godman and the Jewish Messiah but ended up the talisman of a totalitarian empire. Along the way I was transformed from the hero of an allegorical myth into a historical person who expected people to blindly believe in my existence; otherwise, my dad would give them a good going-over after they died."

"Well, I certainly can't see any good reason to believe in your historical existence anymore," affirmed Mary. "No wonder the Literalists had to make blind faith the foundation of their brand of Christianity."

"Actually, we've hardly scratched the surface of the evidence for the mythical Jesus," advised Jesus. "But I can't go into the details here because this is meant to be an engaging satirical romp, not a dusty academic monograph. Anyway, there are plenty of books already out there that contain all the information, and now there are loads of relevant sites on the Internet as well. There's even one for this gospel: **www.thesecondcoming.co.uk**."

"But you said millions of people would come to believe that you were a historical person," complained Peter. "Surely they can't all be wrong?"

"Truth is not decided by a majority vote," said the Lord. "Millions of Romans think that the Emperor is a god, but what do you think?"

"I think he's an arsehole!" said Peter emphatically.

"You see, Peter," continued the Lord, "you quite clearly believe that millions of people *can* be wrong. What you can't believe is that *you* could be wrong—but you're not alone in this. There have been thousands of eminent professors of theology who have suffered from the same sickness, and they're all very well educated and have written lots of books about me."

"There you go!" exclaimed Peter. "It's crazy to suggest that so many great minds are wrong, and this Freke and Gandy you keep on about are right."

And Jesus explained: "No, Peter. It's crazy to believe that a man was born of a virgin, walked on water, and came back from the dead. Compared to that sort of silliness, it's perfectly sane to propose that the Jesus story is a myth that evolved organically from previous Pagan myths.

"The problem is that most theologians are committed Literalist Christians, so they are determined to make the facts fit the theory. Theology is completely different from any other form of academic study because most scholars value rational thought, but the majority of theologians have a set of highly irrational beliefs as the very foundation of their worldview.

"If only there were more scholars with the integrity of the great Albert Schweitzer. He set out to find the historical Jesus but ended up feeling it was a waste of time, because the evidence for my existence just crumbled under investigation. Albert concluded that theologians just created their own Jesuses to suit their preconceptions. He compared it to Jesus emerging from a plastic surgeon's operating theatre, always looking like the person who had worked on him."

Then Jesus added, "I think that's a very perceptive comment because I feel just like a composite of Freke and Gandy right now."

"So everyone is making up their own Jesus," said Mary, thinking that if this was the case, she had done a very good job because her Jesus was really a bit of a hunk.

And the Lord explained, "I am a mythical Everyman so you'd expect everyone to have a different version of me, which of course they do. The Gnostic gospels describe me appearing in all sorts of forms—as a child, an old man, a vision of light. . . . That's because the Gnostics understood that I appear to each person in the form that they're capable of understanding."

And that was when Jesus momentarily morphed into a dead ringer for Timothy Leary, which took everyone by surprise.

Then he announced, "Anyway, that's enough about me. Let's get on to the really exciting stuff."

"But doesn't it make you angry that you've been so terribly misrepresented, Lord?" asked Mary, who was clearly absolutely livid about it.

"Of course I'm angry," replied the Lord. "But I'm not *just* angry, because only love has the power to put things right. You'll understand that when I explain the secret teachings of Gnosis to you."

"But those Literalist bastards caused so much suffering . . . surely they should be brought to justice!" demanded Mary, filled with righteous indignation.

"Revenge doesn't help," explained the Lord. "You'll understand that as well when you get the Gnosis, and I think you're about ready now."

"But I thought the wisdom of Gnosis was lost when those Literalist scumbags burned all the Gnostic gospels!" cried Mary in distress.

"That's true," agreed the Lord, "but a whole library of Gnostic works was discovered in Egypt in 1945, and since then there has been a resurgence of interest in Gnostic Christianity. More recently Freke and Gandy have done an excellent job of recovering the teachings of the Gnosis in their masterpiece, *Jesus and the Lost Goddess.*"

Then he felt he'd better qualify that, so he added, "They've done their best, at least."

Mary looked relieved to hear this, so the Lord continued to steer the conversation in a new direction, saying, "These historical issues about whether I did or didn't exist are all very interesting, but what really matters is the Gnosis. History never saved anyone, but the Gnosis can turn your world inside out!"

"I'm not sure I want my world turned inside out," mumbled Peter, who didn't like the sound of that at all.

But the Lord pressed on regardless, saying, "For the Gnostics, the 'gospel,' which means 'good news,' wasn't the Jesus story itself: It was the message the story contained. The good news is that it's possible to experience Gnosis."

"I'm still trying to get my head around the bad news that you don't really exist!" yelled Peter overemotionally. "And I'm sure there are lots of simple believers like me who will be utterly devastated to discover that the Jesus story is a myth."

And the Lord replied reassuringly, "It can seem like a terrible loss at first, but letting go of irrational superstitions is an important step on the journey to Gnosis. It's sometimes scary when we abandon our safe certainties, but the rewards for embracing doubt are wonderful."

"What do you mean, Lord?" asked Mary.

And the Lord explained, "When we are certain about things, we become closed to new possibilities. When we think we know the way things are, it blinds us to the way things *really* are. Radical doubt is the path to true 'knowing,' or 'Gnosis.'"

Then the Lord concluded, "You see, the thing is this: If someone isn't open to the possibility that Jesus isn't really a person, how will they ever be open to the possibility that they are not really a person? And that's the great secret of Gnosis!"

"What exactly is this Gnosis, then?" asked Mary.

And, with a mischievous twinkle in his eye, the Lord answered, "Gnosis is the experience of stepping out of history and into the mystery."

CHAPTER 9

"Who's up for moving on to some mystical philosophy?" asked Jesus, looking around at the other disciples, but they had all fallen asleep . . . again.

So Mary carried on excitedly, "I'd love it if you'd explain the allegorical meaning of the Jesus story as a journey to Gnosis."

"I'll come to that later," replied Jesus. "First, I'll take a few chapters to elucidate the nature of Gnosis. To begin with, this won't sound as if it has anything to do with Christianity as it's generally understood. But with this understanding when I decode the Jesus myth, it will finally make sense in an amazing new way."

Peter looked skeptical. "I'm rather attached to the traditional old way. I don't see why I can't believe in a historical Jesus and still experience this Gnosis you keep on about."

"You can, Peter," conceded Jesus. "Many people over the centuries have believed in a historical Jesus and also experienced Gnosis. The important thing is that you see that the Literalist claim—that you *must* believe in a historical Jesus to experience salvation—is daft. But it would be equally daft to say that to experience salvation you must *not* believe in a historical Jesus!

"You are not required to believe *anything* to experience Gnosis, because Gnosis is about transcending all your beliefs and directly 'knowing' your own true nature. Most of what we take for knowledge is just opinion. Our opinions make up the story we tell ourselves to make sense of the bewildering business we call life. The way to experience Gnosis is to recognize how profoundly mysterious existence really is."

"I certainly feel pretty mystified right now," said Mary, "because once you've discovered that the most famous man in history didn't really live, you have to ask yourself if there's anything you can be sure of."

"Everything is open to doubt," interjected Thomas sleepily in the background, determined not to miss an opportunity to get on his favorite hobbyhorse.

"Right on, Thomas," said the Lord, nodding in agreement. "And recognizing this is very important, because it is our certainty that traps us in the story."

Then Jesus stated the obvious, saying, "No one really knows what's going on, yet most people act as if they've got the whole caboodle sorted out. Everyone is so engrossed with their story they don't even seem to notice that life is one mother of a mystery."

And that was when the Lord turned to his disciples and roused them from their sleep, saying, "Hey! Wake up, you dozy bunch! Hands up those who think they really know what's going on!"

Then he added, "And I'm asking you the same question, dear reader, except you don't need to put your hand up."

Peter thrust an arm confidently in the air. He was followed hesitantly by most of the other disciples, who had been too sleepy to really take in the question, so thought it best to copy Peter, because they didn't want to look stupid. Big mistake!

"So you think you know what life is, do you?" asked Jesus incredulously.

"We've *all* got our hands up, Lord," announced Peter triumphantly, doing his best to ignore Thomas, who had his arms belligerently crossed, and Dopey, who was still having forty winks—although he doesn't count because he's one of the seven, not one of the twelve.

"Are you *really* sure you understand the nature of existence?" demanded the Lord derisively. "Look at all the incomprehensible suffering and injustice around you everywhere. Look at the vastness of space and the insignificance of a human being. Don't you find yourself even a little perturbed by how strange life is?"

The disciples began to put their hands down—except for Peter, who began waving an arm around like he was bursting to relieve himself, yelling, "I know! I know! I know!"

"What do you know?" asked the Lord.

And Peter answered, "I know that the universe was created by God, and we were made in God's image; and if we're good and do what God says, we'll go to Heaven when we die."

"That's it?" asked Jesus in disbelief. "Does that single sentence really explain the mystery of existence, the miracle of life, the infinite grandeur of the universe?"

Peter felt a bit crushed.

And the Lord explained, "Every story we tell to explain existence is inadequate, because reality is the mystery which pre-exists the story. Unless you understand this, you will never know your own true nature."

"But I already know who I am," insisted Peter.

And Jesus explained, "You are not who you think you are. You are the Imagination that is creating the idea of who you are. You think

59

you are a person called Peter. But in reality, Peter is just a character in this story, and you are much more than that. You are the Author who is imagining the story."

Then the Lord added, "Gnosis is knowing you are the Author. Ignorance is ignoring your true nature and believing you are just a character in the story."

"Are you saying that I'm ignorant?" asked Peter, suspecting that he was being insulted again, although he wasn't entirely sure.

"We're all ignorant while we're lost in the story," explained Jesus.

"I'm not ignorant," maintained Peter. "I know lots of stuff."

"No Peter. You *believe* lots of stuff, usually because other people you meet *believe* the same stuff, but that's not *knowing* for certain."

"I know some things because they are obviously true and beyond doubt," persisted Peter.

"Really? Give me an example."

"The Earth is flat. Everyone knows that."

"But, Peter, right now the reader is probably having a little chuckle at your ignorance, because they are of the opinion that the Earth is a giant ball dangling in empty space. That's the story they tell in their culture; that's their social conditioning."

"It looks pretty flat to me, apart from the hills."

"You're right, Peter, but things are not what they seem to be."

"Okay. The sun goes around the Earth. You can watch that happen every day—that's utterly beyond doubt."

"Again the reader will most likely disagree because according to their story, the Earth is a sphere orbiting the sun."

"That sounds wildly improbable to me."

"You're right," agreed Jesus sympathetically. "And at first the Gnosis sounds even more wildly improbable."

"So what exactly *do* I know?" asked Peter, exasperated.

"It's all very mysterious," interjected Mary.

"Exactly," said the Lord. "And if that's how you feel as a character in this little story, imagine how it must feel to be the reader who exists in the grand story of the physical universe. How mysterious is that?!"

"I don't know. How mysterious is it?" asked Peter, puzzled.

"Infinitely mysterious," explained Jesus. "Get this: Imagine you could count every single grain of sand in the whole world. Well, apparently, the number of stars in the universe is even bigger than that! That really does my head in. The universe is an enigma of mind-boggling proportions. Not just *what* it is, but *that* it exists at all! Anyone who believes they know what's going on is clearly out of their mind."

"That's so true," said Mary, "yet most people take life for granted and carry on as if there was nothing amazing about it."

"But sooner or later," said Jesus, "everyone comes face-to-face with the awesome mystery of existence. It can happen when we're overwhelmed by the beauty of nature or when we're listening to sublime music. It can happen when we witness a baby being born—"

"Or when we fall in love," interjected Mary, looking longingly into Jesus's piercing blue eyes.

Jesus shuffled self-consciously and went on, "But it's often difficult experiences, such as suffering, death, and loss that most powerfully rip open the fabric of the story to reveal new possibilities."

"I can see that," said Mary. "Death is the great doorway into the mystery. Death is the ultimate unknown. We all exit the story in the end, and we don't come back! Present company excepted, of course."

Then Jesus said in his sensitive and caring voice, "Most people have had the experience of waking up all alone in the stillness of the night and facing their mortality. It is at such times that we realize we don't know what it is to be alive. We don't even know who we really are."

"I can't decide if that makes me feel liberated or terrified," confessed Mary.

"It can be terrifying, but it leads to ecstasy," promised Jesus. "*Ecstasy* means 'to step out of oneself.' When you step out of the story of who you think you are, it's an ecstatic feeling of freedom and possibility, because you discover you are the limitless Imagination that is the Author of All. This is the experience of Gnosis."

Then he added, "That's why the Gnostic teacher Montanus said, 'The only true Christianity is ecstasy.' Because *true* Christianity is all about stepping out of the story and experiencing the ecstasy of Gnosis."

It was at this point that Peter disagreed vehemently with the Lord, saying, "Proper Christianity isn't about *ecstasy*, for Heaven's sake! It's about . . . well . . . being proper."

And Jesus answered, "Oh no, Peter, it's much more fun than that."

CHAPTER 10

"**Y**ou said that Gnosis meant knowledge, but now you're saying it's about not knowing!" complained Peter.

"Gnosis is self-knowledge," explained the Lord, "and we only recognize who we really are when we step out of the story into the mystery."

Peter was beginning to feel so mystified that he almost spontaneously experienced Gnosis then and there, but he decided to play it safe and stay confused within the story. So he demanded, "Tell me then, who am I, really?"

And the Lord explained, "We each have two aspects to our identity. In ancient Greek, these aspects are called the *daemon* and the *eidolon.*"

Peter immediately wished he hadn't asked.

Then Jesus continued, *"Daemon* means 'Spirit' or 'essence.' This is what we essentially *are. Eidolon* means 'image' or 'appearance.' This is what we *appear to be."*

Peter began to shuffle restlessly.

And Jesus went on, "In this story you *appear* to be Peter, but that's not who you essentially *are."*

Peter's body language began to shout, *Shut up! I'm not interested!*

And Jesus concluded, "Really you are the Author. You are the Imagination within which everything is arising."

"That's absurd!" exclaimed Peter dismissively. "I'm not imagining this conversation with you and Mary—that's crazy talk."

"I'm not suggesting that 'Peter' is imagining this story," explained Jesus calmly. "'Peter' is part of the story. In reality, there is no 'Peter' who exists as an autonomous individual to imagine anything. There is only the ineffable Imagination of the Author expressing itself as everything and everyone, including Peter, Mary, and Jesus."

"I get it!" enthused Mary. "I am the Author imagining myself to be a particular person called 'Mary.' You are the Author imagining yourself to be a particular person called 'Jesus.'"

"Exactly," confirmed Jesus. "And, by analogy, it is the same for the reader. We are characters within this gospel story; the reader is a character within the life story. They appear to be a person who is reading this book right now. While they are lost in the life story, they will think that this is all they are. But if they step out of their story, they will discover something amazing: In reality everything and everyone is an expression of the one Imagination within which the life story is spontaneously arising right now. This is their essential or 'spiritual' identity."

Then Mary felt confused about something, so she asked, "If we step *out* of the story, does that mean that we're no longer *in* the story?"

And Jesus answered, "You are *both* the Author *and* a character in the story. Gnosis isn't identifying with *either* your essential nature *or* your apparent nature—it is being conscious of *both* poles of your identity. Gnosis isn't escaping from the story into some disembodied existence. It is living within the story of separateness with the knowledge that all is one."

"I've never heard such irrational nonsense," protested Peter. "How can everything be separate and one at the same time?"

And Jesus replied, "To experience Gnosis, you need to transcend either/or logic by grasping the most important concept in Gnostic philosophy—and that's polarity.

"A polarity is a duality of opposites that are essentially one. Examine any polarity and you'll discover that's true. Take 'up and down' for example. Up and down are opposites, yet you can't have 'up' without 'down' or vice versa. Opposites only exist together.

"Polarity is the fundamental structure of reality. This moment exists because the Author is imagining the story, so our existence is predicated on the fundamental polarity of the Primal Imagination and the story it is imagining.

"Because everything is predicated on polarity, everything is characterized by polarity: good and bad, in and out, yes and no, male and female, day and night, waking and sleeping, life and death. . . . You get the idea?

"So it's no surprise that our identity has a polar nature. We are *both* the Author *and* a particular individual in the story. At one pole of our identity, we are the universal Imagination within which everything is arising, so we are one with all; at the other pole of our identity, we appear to be a separate character in the story.

"Philosophies that adopt an either/or approach teach that we are *either* separate *or* all one. Gnostic philosophy is based on an understanding of polarity, so it adopts a both/and approach, teaching that we are *both* one *and* many."

"Gosh!" exclaimed Mary. "I hope the reader is getting this because it's pretty mind-blowing stuff."

"Mind-numbing more like," interjected Peter. "Christianity has nothing to do with *polarity*. It's about God and the Devil."

"Do you think that God might just be another way of talking about what I am now calling the Author?" suggested the Lord in a leading sort of way.

"Definitely not," said Peter, furrowing his brow to give his opinion more gravitas. "God created the world in six days and then took the seventh day off—that's proof that he isn't an author. If he was an author, he'd have done nothing for six days and then rushed off something to meet his deadline at the last moment."

"I think you might be taking things literally again, Peter," cautioned the Lord.

"In the Bible, it says that God created mankind in his own image, so God is obviously a big man," reasoned Peter. "But he's more like a potter than an author, because he fashioned Adam out of clay."

"Can I suggest a different understanding of the same idea?" offered Jesus. "God is the Primal Imagination within which everything is arising. We are images imagined by God."

"Did you hear that, Peter?" exclaimed Mary. "That makes much more sense!"

Unfortunately, what Peter heard Jesus say went something like this: "Blah, blah, blah . . ."

But Jesus went on, nonetheless, saying, "You appear to be an *eidolon,* or image, called Peter, but really we are all the one Spirit, or essence, which is the Primal Imagination, or God."

Peter got the feeling that whatever it was that Jesus was saying was surely blasphemous but couldn't work out if it was possible for Jesus to blaspheme.

Jesus continued, "And what's the difference between the Imagination and the images it imagines? An image can't exist independently of the Imagination, just as a dream can't exist independently of the dreamer. If you look at it one way, they are conceptually distinct, but look at it another way and they are essentially one."

Peter decided that the safest bet was to repeat Psalm 23 to himself, because he always found it reassuringly stirring in times of doubt.

Then Jesus declared, "The problem is that you are so lost in the story of Peter that you believe you are separate from God. But in reality you *are* God."

Peter couldn't remember what came after "the valley of the shadow of death," so he started again from the beginning.

"Don't you get it, Peter?" interjected Mary. "You are both Author and character—*daemon* and *eidolon,* spirit and body, subject and object, essence and appearance, imagination and image, God and man."

Peter caught the last two words, which were the only words that made sense to him. So he conceded, with that slow, patronizing drawl adopted by theologians when they're losing an argument, "I agree that Jesus is both God and man, but not the rest of us. We're just humble folk who look to God for salvation."

"Utter nonsense!" contradicted Jesus impatiently. "The only difference between me and you is that I represent someone who has stepped out of the story and discovered my deeper identity as God. But in reality, we *all* share the same essential or spiritual nature . . . we are *all* God. There is *only* God."

"So I appear to be Mary, but in reality I am God!" exclaimed God as Mary.

"Well, I'm not God—I can tell you that!" mumbled God as Peter.

CHAPTER 11

And thus it came to pass that Peter commented sarcastically, "So Gnosis is believing some incredible theory that contradicts common sense, is it?"

"No, Peter. That's religion," corrected Jesus. "Gnosis is not a theory to be believed. It's a direct realization of your essential nature that manifests as a tangible experience in the body. You know when you've got the Gnosis, because it *feels* good."

"Sounds wonderful!" exclaimed Mary, who was always up for feeling good.

"It *is* wonderful," agreed Jesus. Then he placed his hand gently on his sacred heart and whispered, "Gnosis is a feeling of all-embracing love."

"That's beautiful," enthused Mary, realizing what it was about Jesus that turned her on.

"Go on then, tell us all about love, Mr. Lover-Lover," demanded Peter derisively. "Better still, why don't you invite me to one of those love feasts you run on the quiet?"

"I'll tell you about love, Peter," answered Jesus, "but the love feasts are strictly for those who are liberated from the limitations of the law. Sorry."

Then Jesus uttered words that are very wise but pretty difficult to understand, saying, "Love is what we feel when we see through separateness and recognize our essential oneness."

"That sounds like an overly intellectual definition to me," said Mary, disappointed in Jesus's typically male tendency to reduce feelings to mental abstractions.

"Yeah. I thought love was what you felt when you fancied someone," interjected Peter.

"That's sexual desire," explained Jesus, "which is still a type of love, but it's the desire to become one physically rather than the recognition that we are already one spiritually."

"I think love is something you feel for someone you really like when they're nice to you," asserted Mary.

"That's conditional love," said the Lord. "Often love gets mixed up with all sorts of personal needs, which means we stop loving others when they stop giving us what we need."

"That would explain why I've ended up hating all the men I've ever loved," complained Mary.

"That's understandable, Mary, but real love has nothing to do with liking or disliking someone. Love in its purest form is completely unconditional and never wavers, because it's the recognition of the reality that we are one."

"What do you mean?"

"Let me show you. Think of someone you really love."

"I love you, Lord."

"Great—and I love you, too. But what is it to love someone? You may not have thought about it like this before, but I suggest that love arises when we see through the illusion of separateness and feel one with somebody. When you really love someone, you feel their joys and sorrows as if they were your own. Their happiness makes you happy; their suffering is your suffering."

"That's right, Lord. When you were being crucified, it really upset me because I love you, but I didn't even think about the two crooks who were crucified with you."

"Most people only experience love for a handful of friends and family," explained Jesus. "They feel one with those who are close to them but separate from everyone else."

"I can see that I'm like that."

"But when we realize that we are one with all, our sense of self expands to include everyone and everything. Then we find ourselves in love with everyone and everything."

"Is that why you love everyone—even your enemies?"

"Exactly. I love others *as* my self because I recognize that everyone *is* my Self."

Then Peter interrupted, saying, "I don't see how you can possibly love those Roman bastards who crucified you."

And Jesus explained, "I love and forgive them because I see that they were just playing their roles. If they had realized they were more than just characters in the story, they wouldn't have been able to treat me like that. It was only their ignorance that made them so cruel—they simply didn't know what they were doing."

Then Jesus added, "As I said in the Gospel of Philip, 'Ignorance is the mother of all evil.' When we ignore our essential nature, we think that we're just separate individuals and often act selfishly without regard to the suffering we cause others. But when we discover that all is one, we find ourselves in love with all."

"Sounds good to me," enthused Mary.

"It *is* good, Mary. Think how wonderful it feels to fall in love with one person. Now imagine how wonderful it feels to fall in love with everyone and everything."

"That's big!"

"Yes. Very big!"

"I think I may have experienced this Big Love a few times. It felt fantastic, but I didn't know what it was."

"Most people taste the bliss of Big Love many times in their lives, but without any philosophical context, they don't understand what they have experienced and why, which makes it hard to recapture the experience."

"Does that mean if I understand Gnostic philosophy, I can feel that Big Love again?"

"Absolutely. Gnostic philosophy sets you free from the illusion of separateness and reveals the reality of oneness. This is naturally accompanied by the experience of universal compassion, which the early Christians called *agape.*"

Then Peter confessed dejectedly, "I'm just not brainy enough to understand all this Gnostic philosophy, Lord."

"It's not about being smart, Peter," replied Jesus. "As Paul said, 'It don't matter how much knowledge you've got—if you ain't got love, you ain't got nothing because your Gnosis ain't real.' I'm paraphrasing him, of course, but you get my point."

"That's beautiful, Lord," sighed Mary, feeling a blush come to her cheeks.

And Jesus added in his deepest Barry White voice, "It's all about luuuuuv . . ."

CHAPTER 12

"When you realize that you're really the Author, you can finally love the fact that you're a character in the story," said the Lord.

"So it's okay to love the story, is it?" asked Mary. "You don't have to reject the story to step out of it?"

And Jesus replied, "What's the point of a story you don't get involved with? It's only enjoyable when you enter into it. The problem is that most of us are so lost in the story that it becomes terrifying, but when we are conscious that we exist safely outside the story, we can really enter into the drama of it all."

"That makes sense to me," agreed Mary. "If you know all is one, you can really get into the story of separateness. And let's face it, appearing to be separate individuals is what makes life so good. Look at sex . . . how much fun is that!"

"Exactly," commended Jesus. And then he summed up his point into a pithy one-liner: "The more you can step out, the more you can enter in."

And Mary asked, "Is it like that for the reader?"

So Jesus explained, "The secret to enjoying the life story is for the reader to realize that their essential identity exists outside the story. Then they will feel safe enough to unreservedly dive into their dramas instead of nervously playing in the shallow end of life."

Peter looked skeptical, so Jesus said, "I'll show you what I mean, Peter. Think of a story that you've enjoyed."

"I love Homer's stuff," replied Peter. "Odysseus is a hero I can identify with because we both like messing about in boats."

"Did you find some parts of Odysseus's adventures frightening?"

"When the Cyclops was chasing Odysseus, I was scared shitless."

"Did you enjoy being scared?"

"That was the best bit."

"Why do you enjoy being scared in a story but not in your life?"

"I don't know."

"I think it's because when you read a story, you enter a state comparable to the experience of Gnosis. You identify with Odysseus, which makes it thrilling, but you also realize that you're not really in the story. If you felt you were actually being chased by a one-eyed giant, you would simply be terrified and hate the experience."

"I guess that's right."

"What would happen if you realized that this is a story right now? Maybe you would love even the scary bits? After all, you love telling stories about your bad experiences in the past. I remember when I told you to walk out toward me on the water you were utterly terrified, but now it makes a great anecdote that you love recounting to impress new recruits."

"That's true."

"Maybe if you realize that this is a story, you can love even the bad guys in the adventure because you love the story itself?"

But Peter wasn't sure about that, so he said, "I'm not sure about that. It's all a bit glib. Some events are so horrendous it's impossible to just love the story."

"You're right, Peter," replied the Lord. "Sometimes it *is* impossible to *just* love the story, but it's always possible to *also* love the story. When we are conscious of both poles of our identity, we can suffer as the character but love the story as the Author."

But Peter clearly wasn't satisfied with this answer, so Jesus continued, "When we are lost in the story of separateness, we *just* suffer when things are bad. But if we step out of the story, we can *also* appreciate the beauty that exists in every moment as well—we can embrace the agony *and* the ecstasy within the oneness of being."

Peter still didn't look convinced, so Jesus decided to talk from personal experience because that always makes more of an impact, saying, "For the character Jesus, being crucified was an agonizing experience, but as the Author, I let it happen. Knowing I was the Author allowed me to embrace my terrible fate, because I could see that was the way the story was going. I willingly went along with events as they unfolded—just as the reader is going along with this book . . . although they may not like all that they read!"

Then Peter exclaimed in disbelief, "You were betrayed by your friends and then tortured to death by the people you came to help, for Heaven's sake! Are you telling me you endured all that and still felt love?!"

"The whole point of the Jesus myth is that I am someone who endures the worst yet still loves. I'm an example of what's possible—an ideal to emulate."

"But they put nails through your hands and feet!!!"

"I know, Peter. Some parts of the story are difficult to get through, but it's worth it for the good bits. Anyway, different people appreciate different aspects of the story. The crucifixion scene was awful for me, yet quite a few of the extras in the crowd seemed to have a great day. You see, events in the story are good or bad for different characters. But from the Author's perspective, it all contributes to the drama and what really matters is a good story."

"But they pierced your side with a spear, broke your legs, and played blackjack for your clothes! Surely you can't take that philosophically."

"It *was* truly horrendous. But while the character Jesus was suffering on the cross, I was also conscious of my deeper nature as the Author. The Gnostic Christians symbolized this state by the wonderful figure of the Laughing Jesus. They taught that while I seemed to be suffering on the cross, I was also laughing in the light. This symbolizes the state of Gnosis because when we awaken to all that we are, we can both suffer in separateness and also love being. As I explained in the Acts of John, we can learn to suffer and not to suffer at the same time."

Then Jesus explained, "The figure of the Laughing Jesus is a bit like the Laughing Buddha: Both symbolize someone who has transcended suffering. But without wishing to big myself up too much, I think that the Laughing Jesus is the more powerful image because it pictures someone who is both suffering and not suffering—transcendent *and* immanent, rather than just transcendent like the Laughing Buddha. So it perfectly captures the paradoxical state of simultaneously being in the story and out of it. Freke and Gandy have written an excellent book about it. It's one of my favorites."

"I really like the image of the Laughing Jesus," enthused Mary. "It's much closer to the Jesus I know and love than the traditional image of 'the man of sorrows.'"

But Peter said in a dour voice, "Some things are not a laughing matter."

"I certainly agree that some things should be taken seriously," replied Jesus. "But that doesn't mean we can't *also* find the comedy value of a serious situation, because laughter is a great release. If you take the Gnostic both/and approach, things can be *both* serious *and* funny at the same time—like this gospel. Personally, I enjoy nothing more than poking fun at the things I hold most dear."

But Peter challenged the Lord, saying, "It's all right for you—you're the Son of God. I'm sure anyone born into such a privileged position would find life endlessly amusing. But how do you feel when you're watching the rest of us suffer from your elevated position in cloud-cuckoo-land? How can you love the story when innocent children are starving to death? Surely that's enough to make anyone feel bad!"

A look of deep serenity filled the face of the Lord and he explained, "Love isn't *just* feeling good, Peter. Love is being one with all and suffering with all."

"So when you say you love the story, you still hate all the suffering?" asked Mary.

And the Lord replied, "I hate the suffering because I love the story so much and want everyone else to love it as well."

By this time Peter was looking utterly baffled, so the Lord explained, "I'm not saying we can always *like* what happens in the story. There's plenty in the story of separateness that's simply not very likable. But love is the experience of oneness that transcends all opposites, including liking and disliking. Love is embracing things as they are; and when we embrace things as they are, even the bad things that happen have a certain poignant beauty because they allow us to share love with those around us."

"Oh, Jesus, that's so moving," whispered Mary, wiping away a tear.

And the Lord concluded, "When we realize we are the Author, we transcend the suffering inherent in separateness. Then we can embrace the story as it unfolds and enter into the drama as an embodiment of love."

Then Mary sighed with great relief and proclaimed, "Things really are a lot less frightening when you know that you also exist outside the story. Thank you, Lord. You have shown me that I am safe."

And the Lord shrugged his shoulders and replied, "Jesus saves! That's what I do."

Chapter 13

"**L**ove is the answer! It's a bit of a cliché, isn't it?" mocked Peter. "I think you'll find that the punters are more responsive to fear. We should stick with 'Believe in Jesus or you'll burn in Hell!'"

"That's all a big misunderstanding, Peter," corrected Jesus. "You see, Heaven and Hell aren't places you go when you die—they are ways of experiencing this moment. When we're lost in the story of separateness, life becomes hellish; and when we wake up to oneness, life becomes heavenly—it's as simple as that."

"That can't be right, Lord," objected Peter. "Hell is where those who don't believe in God get tortured forever."

"That's awful," said Mary.

"And Heaven is a place where we get to sing hymns of praise to God for eternity."

"That sounds even worse! Always Sunday morning and never Saturday night!"

"I know it sounds dull, but you do get to look down on Hell and gloat at all those smart-arse philosophers who've been ridiculing Christianity getting roasted."

"How could God sanction torture? I thought he was a loving Father?!"

"God loves his children as long as they do what they're told, and if they don't obey, there's Hell to pay."

"Eternal damnation seems a somewhat severe reprimand."

"God's mean like that. He let his own son be nailed to a tree and didn't intervene, despite being all-powerful."

"That's child abuse!"

"No. That's Christianity—"

Then the Lord interrupted, saying, "You've got it all wrong, Peter. Didn't I clearly state that 'Heaven is within'? So how can it be somewhere that you have to wait until you're dead to visit? Heaven is experiencing Big Love here and now, and Hell is the constant craving for love that we feel when we aren't experiencing Gnosis."

"But what about all the gruesome afterlife tortures?" demanded Peter, feeling a bit let down.

"Hell is always wanting things to be other than they are," continued the Lord. "Hell is the agony of isolation that you experience when you're lost in the illusion of separateness. It's the fear that grips you when you really believe that you're just the person you appear to be because you know that sooner or later, you will inevitably be written out of the story."

"I'm sorry to disagree, Jesus," countered Peter, a little worried that doubting the infallibility of the Lord could undermine his whole theology. "I think you'll find that Heaven is where the faithful are gloriously rewarded with eternal life for holding on to their irrational beliefs, despite all the evidence to the contrary."

"No, Peter. Eternal life is the experience of stepping out of the story. Time is the name we give to the ever-changing sequence of events within the story. The characters exist in time, but our real identity is the Author, who exists outside the story of time. Eternal life is the experience of seeing through time to our timeless, essential nature. You can only experience eternal life right now, because the present moment is where time and the timeless co-exist."

"That's all philosophical bunk! Heaven is where we have a great time forever as recompense for putting up with this lousy world that we're in right now. I can't wait to see those pearly gates myself."

"Funny how all devout believers want to go to Heaven, but nobody wants to die," muttered Mary sarcastically.

"Mock all you like," exclaimed Peter defiantly, "but according to proper Christianity, Hell is where you're punished for living in sin and Heaven is where you go if you repent. That's what I believe, anyway."

"Actually, I agree with you about that," conceded Jesus.

Peter was pleasantly surprised.

"But do you understand what the words *sin* and *repentance* really mean?"

Peter was unpleasantly perplexed.

"The Greek word in the gospels usually translated as *sin* simply means to 'miss the point,' and the Greek word usually translated as *repentance* simply means to 'change perspective.' So we're living in sin when we miss the point of life, and we need to repent by seeing things in a new way—that seems fair enough to me."

"How do we know if we're missing the point?" asked Mary. "What *is* the point of life exactly?"

"I think the point is to be important," offered Peter. "I want to have an enormous basilica named after me, built right on the *Collis Vaticanus* in the center of Rome! How's that for ambition!"

And the Lord explained: "The point of the story seems different to every character. Some crave money, power, and fame; some yearn to help others and change the world; and some just want enough to eat. But underneath these different desires is the same primal desire: We all want to enjoy the show. We all want to love the drama as it unfolds, moment to moment.

"But we can only do that by stepping out of the story of separateness and experiencing Big Love. So we think we want all sorts of different things, but really what we want is to experience Gnosis. That's the real point of this adventure we call life.

"Most of the time we're so busy wanting things to be different in the future that we don't love being in the present—that's 'missing the point' and 'living in sin.' When we miss the point, we don't love being, which is Hell. But if we 'repent' and 'change perspective' by stepping out of the story, then we do love being, which is Heaven."

"I get it!" exclaimed Mary enthusiastically. "When I'm lost in the story of separateness, I think that the point is to do whatever will benefit my character in the story. I become obsessed with my endless selfish desires and miss the point, which is to love being and to embrace everyone and everything with Big Love."

"You've got it," confirmed Jesus. "But I'm not saying we should *only* strive to experience Gnosis and all our other desires are bad. Our desires drive the drama along. Wanting things to be different inspires us to make things better, and that's a good thing. But it's easy to get so distracted by our superficial desires that we miss out on what we really want . . . and that's just stupid."

"So sin is being stupid!" concluded Mary.

And Jesus added, "It's like what I said before: The secret is to first seek the Heaven of Big Love and the rest will all work out for you. I'm paraphrasing again, but you know the quote—it's very famous."

"I've never heard such impractical nonsense!" erupted Peter. "It's like when you told us to give up toiling and be like the lilies of the field. How unrealistic is that?! This philosophy of loafing would clearly lead to complete disaster for both humans and birds."

"I was being *poetic*," explained the Lord defensively. "My point is that it's such a shame to turn existence into an endless grind when the best things in life are free."

"Such as the simple joy of being in the present moment," added Mary.

"Exactly," agreed the Lord. And then, seizing the opportunity to interject another of his famous one-liners, he announced: "You must find the stone that the builders have rejected and make it the cornerstone of your life."

"That sounds like a recipe for a DIY disaster!" exclaimed Peter incredulously.

But Jesus demanded, "Think about it, Peter. What is it that we all reject? Where's the one place we don't expect to find heavenly satisfaction? Here and now. We always think what we're looking for lies in the future, when we hope things will be better. But the present is the cornerstone upon which the future is built. We need to experience Heaven in this moment—and the good news is we can."

And then he added, "As I clearly stated in the Gospel of Thomas, Heaven is laid out over the Earth and people just don't see it. How could I possibly have been talking about a place you go to when you die, if it's laid out over the Earth right now?"

"But you just said that Heaven was inside me," objected Peter, sensing a weakness in Jesus's argument.

"Well, it's *both* inside you *and* outside you," maintained Jesus paradoxically. "I said that in the Gospel of Thomas as well."

Peter looked completely bamboozled, so Jesus added, "That's the point I've been trying to make throughout this chapter. When you look within and discover that you're the Author, the story finally becomes enjoyable because you start to love being—that's Heaven. And when you are lost in separateness, you're missing the point and that's Hell. Heaven and Hell are here and now, depending on whether you're living in sin or willing to repent."

"But the present stinks," countered Peter. "I'm a penniless peasant with a life expectancy of less than forty, living in an occupied country and following a deranged Messiah who doesn't think he really exists! And there are no dentists!!"

"My dear Peter," replied Jesus compassionately, "you're living in Hell because you don't know how to read this moment."

Then he added, "That's another point I made in the Gospel of Thomas."

"I wish you wouldn't keep quoting those Gnostic gospels," complained Peter irritably. "They aren't proper sacred scriptures, you know."

"All the gospels are just books," explained Mary, showing that she'd understood what Jesus had said in the first section of this gospel. "None of them has any special authority."

"But I must say the Gospel of Thomas does have some really good bits," insisted Jesus, because it really was one of his favorites.

Thomas opened one eye briefly, gave Jesus a thumbs-up, and went back to snoozing.

"The Gospel of Thomas is not the Word of God," announced Peter conclusively.

"Are you doubting Thomas?" demanded Mary.

"No. *I'm* Doubting Thomas," piped up a voice in the background.

Chapter 14

hen Peter blurted out, "Look! I don't give a damn about this Gnostic philosophy or about whether Jesus really exists. All I want to know is what happens when I die—is the soul immortal? That's what worries me."

"What *is* the soul, Lord?" asked Mary. "In most of the spiritual books I've read, *soul* is a fudge word used when writers don't really know what they're talking about."

Then Jesus picked up a stick and drew a circle on the ground before them.

And Peter muttered sarcastically, "Here we go again with the doodles in the dirt."

Then the Lord marked a point at the center of the circle and drew a line from the center to the circumference, saying, "The ancients used the symbol of the circle to help us understand that we exist as Spirit, soul, and body. The center represents our spiritual identity, the circumference represents the body, and the radius represents the soul.

"Each one of us is a soul. The soul is our character, and as we've been exploring, our character has a polar nature. On the one hand, a character appears as a particular body in the story, represented by the circumference. But essentially every character is one with the Primal Imagination, represented by the center. The soul, represented by the radius, is the relationship between our essential identity as Spirit and our apparent identity as a body."

Then, much to Peter's dismay, the Lord drew more radial lines connecting the center of the circle with the circumference, saying, "The ancients teach that there are an infinite number of souls arising from our shared spiritual identity at the center of the circle, culminating in different bodies in the world on the circumference. We appear to be separate characters in the story, but at the depths of the soul we are one."

"Sacred geometry is so cool," enthused Mary, "but I still don't really know what the soul *is*. It sounds pretty esoteric."

So the Lord explained, "There's nothing esoteric about it. The word *soul* is a translation of the Greek word *psyche* used by the original Christians. You experience the soul as the psyche, or mind, which connects your experience of appearing to be a body with your essential nature as the 'I' of Spirit."

Peter had never looked more perplexed, so Jesus pointed his stick to the circumference of the circle and explained slowly, "On the surface you appear to be a physical body."

Then he ran the stick up a radial line, saying, "But behind the appearance, you are a psyche or soul."

Finally the stick arrived at the center and the Lord added, "But look deeply within the soul and you'll discover your spiritual identity as the Primal Imagination."

"How can I look into the depths of my soul when I don't understand what the soul is?" asked Peter impatiently. "All this drawing pictures with a stick isn't helping one bit!"

So Jesus said, "Say the word *Peter*."

And Peter said, "Peter."

Then Jesus suggested, "Now think the word *Peter.*"

And Peter thought, *I can't be bothered with this.*

And the Lord explained, "The first 'Peter' was spoken in the outer world of the body, and the second 'Peter' was spoken in the inner world of the psyche."

And Peter thought to himself smugly, *He doesn't know I didn't actually think 'Peter.'*

"I get it!" exclaimed Mary enthusiastically. "My soul is my inner world of thoughts, at the depths of which lies my essential nature as Spirit. That really *is* obvious!"

"Yes," agreed the Lord. "From the perspective of the body on the circumference, the soul appears to be the inner world represented by the radius." Then he added enigmatically, "But from the perspective of Spirit, it's quite different."

"What do you mean?" asked Mary.

And the Lord replied, "Become conscious of being the I of Spirit represented by the center of the circle. Then you will see that your soul is all that you're experiencing right now, represented by the radius extending to the circumference. From this perspective, the soul includes both the inner world of thoughts and the outer world of sensations."

"But I thought the soul was a ghosty thing that would pop out of my body when I died and fly off to never-never land," protested Peter.

And the Lord said, "Peter, the soul isn't really a thing *inside* the body. If I cut open your body and had a look inside, would I ever find your soul? Would I locate a single idea or experience? I don't think so."

Peter had no idea *what* he'd find inside his body and thinking about it made him feel a bit woozy. But that was nothing compared to the nausea that he experienced when Jesus spoke again, saying, "So if the soul doesn't exist in the body, maybe the body exists in the soul?"

"That's what the Platonic philosophers say," commented Mary, flashing her intellectual credentials.

"Well, it's rubbish," asserted Peter. "Anyone can see that the body exists in the world, not the soul."

Then Jesus made matters worse by suggesting, "Perhaps, from the perspective of Spirit, the whole world exists within the soul?"

"You've finally flipped, Lord," concluded Peter. "Looking back I should have seen it coming—all that ego inflation, claiming to be the Messiah; followed by erratic behavior, throwing a tantrum in the temple with the moneylenders; and then the sorry slide into degeneracy: hanging out with whores, tax collectors, and the dregs of society, generally."

But the Lord had learned to ignore hecklers a long time ago at the Sermon on the Mount, so he went on regardless, saying, "From the perspective of the Author, your soul is the story of your character and the world exists as an integral part of the story."

And Peter continued, "I knew you were unstable the moment you cursed that wretched fig tree for no reason whatsoever. What sort of vindictive lunatic curses a fig tree?"

But the Lord just kept on with the show, explaining patiently, "Let me take you through it, Peter. You are able to see your body because it's illuminated by the sun."

"Exactly!" declared Peter belligerently. "The body exists in the world—that's common sense."

"Now close your eyes and imagine your body," suggested Jesus.

And Peter did close his eyes and imagine his body, except he saw himself as a cross between Brad Pitt and Albert Einstein, whereas he actually looked much more like a cross between Homer Simpson and George W. Bush.

Then Jesus asked him, "Is this 'Peter' illuminated by the light of the sun?"

And Jesus answered himself, because he was a bit worried that Peter might get it wrong, saying, "No. The psyche is illuminated by the light of Awareness."

Then the Lord commanded, "Now, Peter, open your eyes and you'll see that the world of the body is *also* illuminated by the light of Awareness. The I of Spirit illuminates everything you experience because if you weren't conscious, you wouldn't be experiencing anything."

Peter opened his eyes and paid attention to the world. As he did so he experienced a sudden rush of colored shapes, vibrant sounds, and ambient aromas.

And Jesus explained, "What we call the world is a series of sensations that exist in the psyche. The psyche or soul is all that's being illuminated by Awareness, including *both* thoughts *and* sensations. So, from the perspective of Spirit, the world exists in the soul."

Peter blinked repeatedly and rubbed his eyes, trying to see what the Lord was saying.

Then Mary exclaimed excitedly, "I get it! My soul is everything that makes up the story of Mary."

"Exactly," commended the Lord. "And how you experience the story depends on your understanding. If your understanding is superficial, you will believe that you're just a body in the world, so that's all you will experience yourself to be. But if you understand that you are essentially the Author, you'll also experience the profound oneness of being, which is the foundation of the story."

And Mary added, "So to experience Gnosis, I need to transform my soul—my story—by deepening my understanding of life."

"Hallelujah!" proclaimed the Lord, throwing his hands up into the air.

"How come Mary always gets it, but I just feel more and more lost?" asked Peter resentfully.

"Don't take it personally," counseled the Lord. "You see, like all Christian gospels, this Gospel of the Second Coming is an allegory about the transformation of the soul. In this parable I represent Spirit, Mary represents the soul, and you, Peter, represent the body. The underlying narrative structure of this gospel concerns the transformation of the soul, symbolized by Mary. Throughout, Mary has become gradually wiser, which has hopefully allowed the reader to deepen their understanding at the same time."

"Well, I'm glad this is making sense to someone," said Peter plaintively, "because I asked ages ago for a straight answer about whether the soul was immortal, but I'm no wiser now than when I started."

"But *I* am," announced Mary in her superior voice. "and that, my dear Peter, is the difference between me and you. I'm the wise soul and you're a stupid arsehole."

CHAPTER 15

"**J**ust tell me what happens when I die, for Pete's sake!" begged Peter.

"Since you symbolize the body, I guess it doesn't look good for you," suggested Mary maliciously.

But Jesus took a more understanding approach, saying, "Peter's concerns about death represent the reader's understandable worries about the mortality of the body. People have all sorts of reasons for reading spiritual books such as this gospel, but deep down it's usually because they want to know what, if anything, happens after death."

"So what does happen after death?" urged Peter. Then he added uncomfortably, "If anything?"

So the Lord explained, "The first thing to recognize is that our essential nature can't die because it was never born. In reality we are the Author who exists outside the story in which we are born and die. The Gnostics called this the discovery of our 'unbornness.'"

But Mary found it a bit of an abstract idea of immortality, so she asked, "If Spirit is immortal and the body is mortal, what about the soul? Do we continue to exist simply as the ineffable oneness of Spirit, or does our individual story also continue in some way?"

And Jesus replied with a question, saying, "What is *Mary?*"

Then he answered himself: "Mary is a set of characteristics that has taken on a separate identity as her character has developed over time. Mary is an evolving idea in the Imagination of the Author. The Author expresses the idea of Mary as a particular figure in the story, and what she does and says as a body shows us the characteristics of her particular soul or psyche. Mary's actions arise from her psyche, because the story she tells about life defines her motivations.

"Mary is a possibility imagined by the Primal Imagination so when Mary's body dies, that's not necessarily the end of the story. Perhaps when we die as a character in one story, we're recast in another story. Maybe we become a new person based on the previous part we were playing, in a new situation that offers new opportunities for continued character development. The possibilities are endless because the Author's Imagination is limitless."

"Is it really possible that I'll continue to exist as a soul without this particular body?" asked Mary uncertainly.

"Why not? You do at night when you dream," replied Jesus buoyantly. "In your dreams, you often appear to be someone else in a different world—your body is coming and going from your experience all the time."

"Are you talking about reincarnation?" asked Peter suspiciously. "That's not a very Christian idea."

"It's a perennial teaching embraced by the Gnostic Christians, and I see no reason to just dismiss it," asserted Jesus. "After all, I was killed off and I came back!"

"I don't want to come back to this lousy world," complained Peter petulantly. "I like the traditional theory that when we die, we go to meet our Maker in Heaven."

And the Lord explained, "You can merge with the Maker right now, as soon as you become conscious of your deeper nature, and that will be heavenly—I know this because I've done it."

"I would have thought that facing the death of the body was enough to make anyone want to step out of the story and experience their deeper nature," suggested Mary cheerfully.

"I would have thought so, too," agreed Jesus. "And when you explore the depths of the soul, you realize that you are, and have always been, and will always be, a possibility in the Imagination of the Author."

"I'm warming to the idea that when this body dies, I reincarnate for the sequel," interjected Peter, concluding that anything was better than nothing.

Then he added theatrically, "In *Peter Rides Again,* I'm not going to be an illiterate fisherman living in a backwater like Palestine. I'm going to have wealth and power and live in my own little walled city right in the heart of Rome."

"I can see it now," said Jesus regretfully. "You'll be a high-powered executive running a multinational religious cult."

"I wonder who I was in my previous lives. I'm sure I was really famous . . . Cleopatra perhaps?" said Peter, beginning to find the reincarnation thing so exciting that he gave away his secret predilection for cross-dressing.

"I think that *I'm* more likely to have been Cleopatra," replied Mary, trying to remove from her mind the strangely arousing image of Peter as an Egyptian queen.

And Jesus interjected, "Half of the women I've ever met have claimed to be the reincarnation of Cleopatra."

Then he added, "And the other half claimed to be the reincarnation of you, Mary!"

And Mary mused, "Funny how no one ever remembers being a toilet cleaner."

Suddenly Peter wasn't so sure about reincarnation, and he felt the uncomfortable feeling of uncertainty that he really hated. So he gave a plaintive cry for reassurance and pleaded, "Lord, can you please promise me that I won't die when I die? That's all I really care about."

And the Lord replied, "While we're in this story, what may exist in another story is only a possibility. Gnostic philosophy can't prove that the soul will live on in a new story when the body dies in this one—it can only show us the way things are right now. But once we become conscious of the depths of the soul, we can at least see there's no reason to suppose that death won't simply be another transformation in the flow of experiences that make up the story of the soul."

"That all sounds pretty tentative," complained Peter fretfully. "I just want to know for sure if there's going to be something or nothing after I kick the bucket."

"Can you imagine nothing?" asked the Lord.

Peter thought about it and realized *nothing* was the one thing that he really couldn't imagine.

And Jesus continued, "You can't imagine nothing because you're always there to imagine it. You simply can't imagine not being; you can only imagine different ways of being. So, perhaps, you can never be nothing—you have to be in some way or the other."

"Perhaps . . . maybe . . . probably," drawled Peter suspiciously. "Some certainty wouldn't go amiss."

So Jesus explained, "There's no certainty about death, because death is an encounter with the absolute mystery of existence. Whatever we may think is going on while we're alive, we're all destined for a date with death. We're heading from different directions toward the same destination . . . and its nature is a mystery."

Then Peter begged in desperation, "Just tell me, Lord! Will you or won't you grant me eternal life—like you said you would?"

And that was when Jesus announced, "I'm not here to grant you life after death. I'm here to make sure that you experience life *before* death. The important thing is really living now."

"Fair enough. I'm with you, but will there always be a now for me or could Peter come to nothing?"

"If there's nothing, you won't be there to experience it, so there isn't anything to worry about."

"I'm quite attracted to the idea of reincarnation, but it seems a bit irrelevant if I don't remember being Peter in my next life."

"Stop worrying about it. When you fall in love with the moment, what happens when you die really doesn't matter at all."

"It matters to me, all right!"

"All that matters is what state you leave the story in. Will the story be better for you having played your part?"

"I don't care about *the* story; I just care about *my* story. I want to be clear about what to expect."

"Trust the Author to come up with something good, and concentrate on enjoying your life here and now. Then, if it does all end, at least you've enjoyed it while it lasted. And if it continues, that's brilliant!"

"But you seem to be the Author's spokesman on these matters—surely you can tell me how things are going to turn out."

"It will spoil the story if you know how it ends. Death is meant to be a mystery because it reminds us that life is also an unfathomable mystery. Death is the doorway out of the story into the mystery. That's why those who ignore death end up stuck in their story, but those conscious of death experience the mystery now."

As Jesus was clearly intent on telling him nothing, Peter turned in desperation to Mary, saying, "You're supposed to represent the soul. Can you tell me what it will be like when I'm dead?"

And Mary answered optimistically, "Jesus says that stepping out of the story is the experience of ecstasy, so I expect death will be pretty ecstatic! If the climax of sex is *la petite mort,* what must *la grande mort* be like, because that's the climax of life?!"

And so it came to pass that Mary gave Jesus a flirty little wink and he went pink all over. Then, with a line that begs to be put on a T-shirt, she announced:

> "Death is coming.
> Life is foreplay."

CHAPTER 16

Peter was getting so mad listening to all this heresy that he could have cut someone's ear off. So he announced sarcastically, "This is meant to be a Christian gospel, but none of what you've been saying has anything to do with proper Christianity. Proper Christianity is about believing that Jesus is the Christ who died for the sins of the world."

"I'm afraid that's another misunderstanding, Peter," explained Jesus. "Actually, as Paul said, it's about becoming the Christ yourself by experiencing Christ Consciousness."

"Is that another way of talking about Gnosis?" asked Mary.

"Exactly," said Jesus. "The Christ symbolizes our spiritual nature. It's another name for what Hindus call the Atman, Buddhists call the Buddha nature, and each one of us calls I. The Christ is the one 'I-in-All.'"

"I get it," interjected Mary. "We experience Christ Consciousness when we become conscious of our essential nature, which is represented mythologically by the figure of the Christ. So anyone conscious of their essential nature *is* the Christ!"

"That's it," confirmed Jesus. "So, as Paul said in his Letter to the Romans, you can only truly call yourself a Christian if you experience Christ Consciousness."

Then he added provocatively, "And that reduces the number of so-called Christians from two billion to just a small handful!"

"I thought a Christian was someone who believed that Jesus was the Christ," protested Peter.

"I *am* the Christ because I represent someone who has awoken to oneness," explained Jesus. "As I made clear in the excellent Gospel of Thomas, 'I am the one who lives from the undivided.'"

By now Peter was so bewildered that he really didn't know what was happening, which was a great step forward.

So Jesus told him straight, "It's like this, Peter: I am the Christ and so are you, if you did but know it."

"But if I'm really the Christ, how come I feel so confused?" asked Peter a little pathetically.

"That's because you have two aspects to your nature," explained Jesus long-sufferingly. "On the one hand, you're Peter, a character in this story who's a bit stupid and often confused—that's what you appear to be. But if you become conscious of your spiritual or essential identity, you'll discover that you are the Christ."

Then he added, "Christianity is all about becoming conscious of what Paul calls 'the Christ within.'"

"What's this, Lord? Are you now saying you exist inside me?" exclaimed Peter with a self-conscious shudder. "That's just weird!"

"Listen carefully, Peter, and I'll explain. Christianity teaches the path of initiation that leads to self-knowledge or Gnosis. Gnostics call the first stage the 'psychological' or 'soul' initiation, because it involves looking within and exploring the 'psyche' or 'soul.' This is the process of personal growth that occurs when we really start to ask 'Who am I?'

"At first, we hear this as questioning what sort of character we are, so we start to explore our psychological nature to find out. But as our exploration of the soul becomes more profound, we start hearing the question 'Who am I?' in a new way. We've been on a quest to improve our character, but now we begin to wonder whether we really are *just* a character in the story.

"The second stage of the path to Gnosis is called the spiritual initiation because it leads to the discovery of our Spirit. It involves looking deeper within and finding our essential identity—the mysterious presence each one of us calls 'I,' which is witnessing the body and the psyche. The 'I' is the Christ within. This is our shared spiritual nature, for there is, in truth, only one 'I': the Author."

"This is becoming real clear now," said Mary. "Gnosis is stepping out of the story of separateness and recognizing that we are all one."

"So it's all about being some huge amorphous blob is it?" asked Peter, finding the whole idea of oneness increasingly unattractive.

"Becoming one with the Christ isn't being assimilated into the Borg, for goodness' sake!" exclaimed the Lord, beginning to lose his patience. "Quite the opposite. Recognizing that all is one makes you a much more interesting individual. Take me as an example— my character has kept people fascinated for centuries.

"The truth is, the more we recognize our essential nature as the infinite possibilities of the Primal Imagination, the more we can fulfill our potential as a particular person in the story. And this is because the more a character realizes that he or she is actually the Author, the more the Author really gets into the character, so the more rounded out that character becomes.

"The irony is that in order to wake up to oneness, we need to become more of an individual. The psychological initiation involves 'individuating,' as that great modern Gnostic Carl Jung called it.

We initially develop as a character in the story by learning from the culture around us. Spiritual awakening begins when we start to doubt our conditioning and explore our own insights. Then, as we become independent freethinkers, we separate ourselves from the herd, who are stuck repeating the same old thoughts over and over again.

"One of the great allegorical messages in the Jesus myth is 'Follow your heart, not the herd.' I represent someone with the courage to be true to myself, whatever the personal consequences. Compare that to the behavior of the mob: On Palm Sunday, they all turned out to cheer as I entered Jerusalem, but by Easter they were baying for my blood. That's mass mind for you—very unconscious.

"We need to individuate as a separate *some-one* before we can become conscious of the *All-One*. That's what the psychological initiation involves. This prepares us for the spiritual initiation that leads to the experience of Christ Consciousness. Then we can live as a some-one in the knowledge that it's All-One. We can consciously be 'in the story but not of it,' to slightly misquote myself."

CHAPTER 17

"Okay, that's most of the philosophical background covered, so now we can start on the mythological section of this gospel," proclaimed the Lord. "Let those with ears hear."

"I've got ears!" affirmed Mary enthusiastically.

"Not if I chop them off," muttered Peter darkly.

"Gnostic mythology is about God the Father and God the Son," pronounced Jesus.

"Yeah. We know all that," complained Peter.

"And the Mother Goddess and her Daughter," continued Jesus.

It was at this point that Mary squealed with delight and Peter put his fingers in his ears.

And the Lord explained, "You see, Mary, when the first Christians transformed the Pagan myth of the dying and resurrecting Godman into the myth of Jesus, they also borrowed the Pagan myth of the lost and redeemed Goddess."

"Wow! This is going to be good," enthused Mary. "Tell me more."

And the Lord did tell her more, saying, "God is the Author and the Goddess is the life story. She is all that's being imagined by the Primal Imagination. That's why the Gnostics sometimes call her Zoë, meaning 'Life.'"

"Far out!" exclaimed Mary in a state of mythological rapture.

"In Gnostic mythology, the Goddess has two aspects that correspond to the Pagan goddesses Demeter the Mother and Persephone her Daughter. The Mother represents the whole of the life story—the universe, the nature of things; the Daughter represents a character's individual story—an individual life. So the Goddess represents the whole and each part: the universal soul and each individual soul."

"Fabulous!" gushed Mary in a state of metaphysical bliss.

"God the Father is the one Awareness that's dreaming up the whole story, and the Son is Awareness conscious of the particular story of an individual character. The Son is the 'I' of our essential nature—the Christ within."

"Awesome!" shrieked Mary in a state of speculative ecstasy.

Then Jesus started to go into the big picture, grandly pronouncing, "The Gnostics compared God to light because light illuminates everything but is itself invisible. They pictured the Primal Imagination, paradoxically, as a Dazzling Darkness. If there's only light, with no objects to reflect on, it would be dark. In the same way, God is the Primal Imagination that's imagining everything, but if there were no images to be conscious of, it would be unconscious."

"So before the beginning of the story, the Primal Imagination is unconscious because it's not thinking about anything," suggested Mary, keen to participate.

"Exactly. So what does it do?"

"I don't know . . . what does it do?" replied Mary in nervous anticipation.

"I'll give you a clue. In the beginning was the word . . ."

"I get it! The Author makes up the story."

"Precisely. In the beginning was the story, and the story was within the Author and the story was the Author."

"I hear what you're saying! When the Primal Imagination is imagining nothing, it isn't conscious that it exists. So it imagines what it is in order to become conscious of what it is."

"You're hearing me. The Primal Imagination dreams up infinite stories to explore its limitless potential."

"God is in search of himself through his creation," proclaimed Mary as a punch line.

Then she added as a double whammy, "The Author discovers who they are through their work."

"But this is the predicament," cautioned Jesus. "There's one Awareness imagining that it is experiencing the life story from the perspective of all the different characters it's dreaming up. But, as in a dream, Awareness has become lost in its own imaginings, convinced that it is each of the characters it's imagining itself to be."

"I see where you're going. The Primal Imagination is imagining the life story so that it can come to know itself and love the story, but it keeps mistaking itself for the separate individuals it's creating. And when it gets engrossed with the suffering of separateness, the story doesn't seem very good at all."

And Mary added optimistically, "So the Primal Imagination has dreamed up Gnostic philosophy to help it understand its true nature."

"That's it!" verified Jesus excitedly. "That's why the Author of All has dreamed up this book, which the reader is reading right now."

Then in an audacious bid to grab the reader's full attention, Jesus pressed his point home, saying, "The reader is a character within the life story. While they're convinced that they're just the person they appear to be, they'll remain lost in the story of separateness. But when they get the Gnostic message, they'll recognize their essential identity as the Author of All. Then they'll experience Gnosis and be filled with Big Love—they will love being."

"And that's the purpose of life!" declared Mary. "Because when we love the story, the Author loves the story."

And so it happened that Jesus brought a certain pathos to his voice and whispered softly, "Deep down we all long to love being. It's only when we're in love with life that the hollow feeling inside is filled, and our constant craving gives way to satisfaction. But when we're lost in the story of separateness, we look for love in all the wrong places. We expect to find satisfaction in the world, but everything is impermanent and any fleeting satisfaction is soon replaced by a new desire; that is, until we realize that what we really long for is to know our true nature. And when we do, we simply love being what we are."

"I get goose bumps all over when you say that, Jesus."

"I'm not surprised. You see, these teachings are encoded in the Christian myth of the Goddess. And in the Jesus story, you symbolize an aspect of the Goddess."

"This is fantastic! One minute I've never heard of the Christian Goddess, and the next I find that I *am* the Goddess!"

"She's called Sophia, which means wisdom because this is what she comes to embody."

"That's a lovely name. What's Sophia's myth about?" asked Mary, captivated.

"It's a terrifying tale with a feel-good ending that is found in various Gnostic gospels, such as 'The Book of the Soul,'" replied the Lord.

And lo! The Lord gave unto them a potted version of the Christian myth of the Goddess, saying, "Sophia is living with her Father, but then she goes looking for love and ends up in a real bad state, getting abused and raped and eventually falling into prostitution. She realizes that she's living in sin and repents. She calls to her Father for help, and he sends Jesus down to rescue her from suffering. Then Jesus and Sophia get married and live happily ever after."

"What a romantic story," cooed Mary.

"And a lot more believable than the Jesus myth because—let's face it—that's fantasy fiction from beginning to end."

"Does the myth of Sophia have an allegorical meaning?"

And the Lord explained: "It tells the story of the soul getting lost in the story of separateness and then being redeemed through Gnosis. When the Primal Imagination conceives of a character, it enters the story as a person in search of fulfillment. This is represented by Sophia, who leaves her Father's home and ventures into the world looking for love in all the wrong places.

"The soul has arisen from the unconscious oneness of the Primal Imagination and longs for the conscious oneness of Gnosis, but it has become lost in the story of separateness. So the soul suffers until it realizes that it's 'missing the point' and 'changes perspective,' which is represented by Sophia acknowledging that she's in trouble and turning to God.

"God the Father responds to Sophia's call of distress by sending his Son, who rescues her. This is telling us that the individual soul is saved from suffering in separateness when it recognizes its essential nature, symbolized by the Christ."

By this point, Peter felt so appalled by what he was trying hard not to hear that he pulled his fingers out of his ears, yelling, "Proper Christianity has got nothing to do with a Goddess!"

Then he added, with a defiant pelvic thrust, "We're strictly 'God has a dick!'"

CHAPTER 18

"We're finally in a position where I can start to explain the allegorical meaning of the Jesus myth," announced Jesus portentously. "As you may remember in the New Testament gospels, I mainly teach in parables, the meaning of which I promise to reveal to my disciples later."

"Yeah. That's right. And you never do tell us—that really ticks me off," complained Peter.

And the Lord answered, "That's because my job then was to point to the hidden meaning that would be revealed during the process of initiation by a living Gnostic master when the initiate was ready. And that's exactly what I'm going to do now."

So the Lord began, "Let's start with an overview of the symbolic structure of the general narrative. I'm an Everyman figure who represents, well, everyone. And my story encodes teachings about the process of initiation through which every initiate comes to Gnosis.

"I am born as God incarnate. That sounds impressive, but we're all God incarnate, as I hope you can now see. We are all the Primal Imagination imagining itself to be a particular character in the life story.

"The first major symbolical event in the Jesus myth is my baptism, representing the psychological initiation. I'm washed clean, which symbolizes the initiate purifying themselves psychologically from everything that keeps them stuck in the story and so being reborn as a new person on the path to self-knowledge.

"My crucifixion and resurrection represent the spiritual initiation. They symbolize the initiate dying to the idea that they're just a separate individual and coming to life as someone who recognizes their true essential nature as the Author."

"An elegant interpretation of the conceptual architecture of the piece," applauded Mary.

"Thank you," said Jesus. "Now let's look at some of the allegorical detail. To start at the beginning, the myth of my nativity represents the process through which we come into existence as a character in the life story. I'm born at the solstice because this is the turning point of the year, when the days start getting longer and the light returns. I am the light of Awareness coming into the world—we all are. That's why my story begins with a star, which is an archaic image. The Egyptians believe that everyone is actually a star."

"Those Egyptians are completely nuts!" announced Peter xenophobically. "They've got a crocodile-headed hippo as their goddess of childbirth! How mad is that?!"

"Plato mentions the star thing in the *Timaeus*," interjected Mary, who had a classical education, which isn't as impressive as it sounds, because there wasn't any other type of education available in the ancient world.

"I think you'll find that I mention the idea myself in the recently published Gospel of Judas," inserted Jesus.

At which Judas piped up with, "I'm sorry, mate—you can't go there. I've sold the rights to my gospel to *National Geographic*. Reprints by permission."

And Mary snarled, "It's all about money with you, Judas."

"Yeah," growled Peter. "Sellout!"

And Judas complained, "Look, I've been misrepresented. My gospel sets the record straight—it's all in there. I'm really a good guy!"

"Go hang yourself!" yelled Mary.

It was at this point that the narrator realized this chapter was wandering way off topic and asked Jesus to get things back on track.

The Lord obliged because he was very accommodating like that, saying, "The idea that we're really a star is absurd if you take it literally, but if you understand it poetically, it's quite beautiful. The ancients pictured the Goddess as the night sky covered in stars, which they compared to a veil. Stars were seen as holes in the veil through which the light of God shone into the world of appearances. So each one of us is like a star, because we are all like holes in the veil of appearances."

"What do you mean?" asked Mary, intrigued.

"When you look into someone's eyes, you see a black hole surrounded by colored patches. But when you look through the appearance, you connect with something you can't see."

"Awareness!" announced Mary.

"Precisely. The eyes are like windows through which we can glimpse the light of someone's essential nature, which exists beyond the appearance."

"We're openings in the veil through which shines the Dazzling Darkness of Awareness."

"That's right. So the Jesus myth starts with a star that represents my essential nature, shining above the cave in which I am born."

"I thought you were born in a stable," objected Peter petulantly. "According to the Gnostics, I was born in a cave," explained Jesus.

"The cave is an ancient symbol that represents the universe."

"If you take a look at the night sky, you can see how you could easily picture it as the vault of an enormous cave," urged Mary.

Then Jesus announced, "I am the light of the world, the Dazzling Darkness, born into the cave of the universe. So when I am born, the cave is filled with light."

"It doesn't say any of this in the Jesus story," complained Peter.

"It does in the Gnostic gospels," explained Jesus.

And then he continued, "The cave that I'm born in is Plato's cave."

"But you were born in Bethlehem, Lord," argued Peter. "What's Plato's cave doing in Bethlehem?"

"It's a literary allusion, Peter. Plato's myth of the cave is an ancient allegory that's a prototype for the Jesus story."

"What?! Christianity is based on Plato?" cried Peter in disbelief.

"Actually, Plato probably borrowed the myth of the cave from the Pythagoreans, and they probably got it from Egypt," explained Jesus. "It's a very old story."

"What's it about?" asked Mary eagerly.

"Plato compared our predicament to that of prisoners stuck in a cave, watching the shadows cast by the light outside. He imagined someone escaping the cave into the light and then returning to set the others free by explaining that they were entranced by shadows. With cynical wit, Plato suggested that such a 'just man' would be resented and put to death by his fellows. He wrote: 'The just man will have to endure the lash, . . . and finally, after every extremity of suffering, he will be crucified.'"

114

"But that's what happened to you, Lord!" exclaimed Peter incredulously.

"I know," agreed Jesus. "It makes me feel like a remake of an old classic."

Then he added, "Elsewhere, Plato refers to the 'Son of God' being 'crucified in the Cosmos.'"

"That's just got to be more than a coincidence," asserted Mary.

"Of course it is. You see, I represent each one of us who's born a prisoner in the cave of the cosmos, but I escape and step out into the light. When I come back to tell others that they can also escape, however, everyone is really pissed with me—so they do me in."

"I can see why they'd want to do that," mumbled Peter to himself.

Then Jesus said, "According to the Neoplatonic philosopher Plotinus, Christianity is about 'the ascent from the cave.'"

"Christianity has got nothing to do with ascending from caves," grumbled Peter under his breath.

"You're wrong, Peter," replied Jesus, who had excellent hearing. "You see, I was born in the cave of the universe as a separate individual. Then, when I experienced the spiritual initiation, represented by my death and resurrection, I ascended out of the cave to the Dazzling Darkness."

"So that's why when I went to the cave that was your tomb, I found it empty," said Mary.

"That's right, Mary," affirmed Jesus. "You represent the wise soul who recognizes that the cave of the cosmos is empty because in reality, we exist outside the cosmos as the Dazzling Darkness."

"So the Jesus story starts with your birth in a cave and ends with the empty cave," concluded Mary.

"Precisely," agreed Jesus. "Now, do you remember what happened the moment I died and ascended from the cave?"

"The veil in the temple ripped," answered Mary.

And Jesus explained, "The veil in the temple of Jerusalem was a tapestry of the starry night sky. The veil represents the Goddess, the life story—the way things seem to be."

"I get it!" proclaimed Mary. "The veil of appearances was torn open. You escaped Plato's cave, leaving the land of shades, and went into the light."

"That's Gnosis!" proclaimed Jesus.

Then he added considerately, "The reader may find the reference to Plato's cave a bit esoteric. If they happen to be a movie lover, it may help if I suggest that the cave is like the Matrix, I'm a bit like Neo, and Gnosis is similar to taking the red pill."

"Now what are you talking about?" asked Peter.

So the Lord explained, "This stuff isn't for you, Peter, it's for the reader. They'll almost certainly understand my references to *The Matrix,* just as all educated people in the ancient world would have understood the references to Plato's cave in the Jesus story."

Then he concluded, "If you want to understand all of the clever little references to other myths in my story, you should check out Freke and Gandy's *Jesus and the Lost Goddess,* which forensically examines everything I'm touching on in this gospel."

"From what I can tell, this whole gospel is just a rehash of Freke and Gandy's previous books," muttered Peter derisively.

"Yes," admitted Jesus. "But with added gags."

Chapter 19

nd then the Lord spoke again, saying, "Okay, after my nativity, the next major event is my baptism, representing the psychological initiation through which an initiate begins the journey of self-knowledge. What happens next? Can you remember?"

"You wander into the wilderness, where you're tempted by the Devil," replied Mary.

"Correct," commended Jesus. "In the same way that God represents oneness, the Devil represents separateness. So I'm lured by the possibility of inflating my separate identity and believing that I'm something special as an individual, rather than transcending separateness and recognizing that I'm really the Author. I'm tempted to understand the teaching 'You are God' as meaning that the person I appear to be is God, rather than humbly acknowledging that the person is just a character in the story."

"Is that a test that all initiates face?" asked Mary.

"Yes," replied Jesus. "Of course, I pass with flying colors, as you'd expect. And the next thing I know, I'm a controversial guru making a big splash on the spiritual lecture circuit."

Then the Lord explained, "During this period, I attempt to get across the basics of the Gnostic teachings and expose the religious authorities as frauds who have thrown away the keys to Gnosis. The Jewish religion has endless rules and regulations about the most stupid things, but I boldly declare that there are only two commandments and the second is pretty much like the first.

"The first commandment is to love God, which means be one with the Primal Imagination, and the second commandment is to love others as your self because when you realize all is one, you know everyone is your Self."

And Mary interjected, "I can't see how you could have gotten the message across any more simply than that!"

Then Peter asked impatiently, "When do I come into the story, Lord?"

"Yes, tell us, Jesus. What was all that 'chosen few' thing about?" complained Mary irritably. "I can't help feeling that it was a real mistake making all twelve of your inner circle men. Not only is it chauvinist, but men were guaranteed to take your spiritual teachings and use them to justify world domination. Women are so much more evolved. Naked men still look like monkeys, for Heaven's sake! I should know—I've seen a fair few."

And the Lord explained, "I'm surrounded by twelve disciples because they represent the twelve signs of the zodiac, and I represent the polestar around which the constellations turn like an enormous wheel. That's why I meet my disciples in Galilee, which means 'wheel.'

"The ancients call the zodiac the Wheel of Necessity because it represents the relentless cause and effect of the material universe, which governs our individual fate. When we're lost in separateness, we're caught on the wheel and then we suffer. That's why Pythagoras calls it the Wheel of Grief.

"The reader might appreciate it if we update the image and think of it as the Ferris Wheel of Joy and Suffering. Everyone in the story experiences times when they feel up and times when they feel down. Everything is going our way, and then suddenly we're feeling completely lost. But this doesn't last for long because we start going up again—until down we go, and so on and so on . . . until we glimpse another possibility."

"What's that?" asked Mary eagerly.

And the Lord replied, "We see that we aren't really stuck on the wheel at all. Because at the still center of our being, we are the Christ, symbolized by the polestar around which the universe moves.

"In the Jesus myth, I represent someone who has stepped out of the story and recognized their true nature as the Author. My twelve disciples represent different states of being lost in the story of separateness, or stuck on the wheel. That's why Judas betrays me for money, Peter denies me because of fear, Thomas doubts me because of a lack of understanding . . . you get the idea?"

"I get it completely," announced Mary. "The disciples are men because they're meant to be stupid."

Peter said nothing and that was the most intelligent thing he had said all day.

So Jesus explained, "The ancients imagined the wheel like a sundial. At the center is the gnomon, the arm of the sundial, which casts a shadow that rotates around the circle, marking out the twelve hours of a day. In this analogy, the gnomon represents the Christ, the Atman, the Buddha nature, the 'I' of Spirit. The shadow that the gnomon casts represents the *eidolon* or image, the separate self. The circle that the shadow traces is the Wheel of Time, represented in the Jesus myth by my twelve disciples."

119

"So how do I fit into the story?" asked Mary in breathless anticipation.

And Jesus answered, "If you remember the Sophia myth, you'll recall that my mission is to rescue the soul from suffering in the story of separateness. And the lost soul is symbolized by you, Mary."

"That sounds about right," conceded Mary. "At this point in my character's development, I was pretty lost in the world, looking for love in all the wrong places. As I remember it, I was still a working girl at Delilah's Bordello, which is where I met Peter for the first time—but that's another story."

"There are already too many apocryphal Christian stories without you introducing new ones now, Mary," cautioned the Lord. "The point is that, like Sophia in the myth, you're a fallen woman and I've come to rescue you."

"I'm the damsel in distress and you're my knight in shining armor."

"Except I'm a pacifist who rides a donkey."

And then Peter demanded, "What sort of pacifist rampages through the temple attacking moneylenders?!"

"A pacifist who knows how to kick butt when necessary," answered the Lord with a swagger.

Then he explained, "My Father's House represents Awareness. I saw that Awareness was filled with lust for money, so I decided to sort things out. It's an allegory representing the process of psychological transformation that all initiates must undergo in order to free themselves from the selfishness that traps them in separateness. Everything I do is allegorical."

"That's a lame excuse, Lord," scoffed Peter. "I think you just lost the plot."

"I assure you that righteous anger is sometimes part of the plot. I got angry because everyone was so lost in separateness that they were all trying to make a profit from one another instead of loving each other. So I put a stop to it. It's a superhero's job to dis the villains—I'm sure that Batman would have done the same."

Then the Lord continued reflectively, "Except Batman would have used more gadgets because he's one of the few superheroes without any superpowers. Of course, I've got plenty. I can give sight to the blind, raise the dead, and battle with demons—all of which represent helping those lost in ignorance to experience Gnosis."

This was pretty confusing for Mary and Peter, because they had no idea that Jesus had a secret passion for Marvel comics, which are in the same genre as his own story.

So the Lord explained, "Jews are really good at creating superheroes. There's Superman, created by Jerry Siegel and Joe Shuster; Batman, created by Bob Kane and Bill Finger; and Spider-Man, created by Stan Lee and Jack Kirby. All Jews! And then there's me—the greatest Jewish superhero of them all, created way back in the first century and still playing in cinemas everywhere nearly two millennia later."

"I've never heard of any of these strange Godmen that you're talking about. Can they battle with demons like you?" asked Peter. "Because the most exciting times for me were watching you vanquish demons. Awesome, dude!"

And Jesus remarked, "The idea of demonic possession is a bit outdated. Demons represent those parts of our character that keep us stuck in separateness, and the psychological initiation is the process of dealing with your demons."

"No wonder you had to exorcise seven demons from Mary," sneered Peter. "She's so neurotic—I'm surprised there weren't more."

And that was when Jesus realized this had neatly brought the conversation back to Mary, whom they had been discussing before the rather surreal digression into Marvel comics.

So he explained, "The ancients taught that we had to go through seven stages in the process of coming to self-knowledge. They were represented in the ancient world by the Dance of the Seven Veils, in the course of which the dancer revealed their naked self."

"I remember watching Mary do that number at Delilah's," interjected Peter excitedly, "and it was hot—I can tell you!"

"The point is I helped Mary through all the required seven levels," insisted Jesus, blushing.

"That was so *sweet* of you," giggled Mary.

"That was how you came to represent the wise soul," explained Jesus.

"And was that when I anointed you with oil?" asked Mary.

"Yes," replied the Lord, "but I don't think that's got any allegorical significance. I just asked for that to be in the story because I thought I'd enjoy it . . . and I deserved a treat with all that suffering coming up."

"But Christ means 'the Anointed,'" objected Mary.

"Does it?" exclaimed Jesus. "What an extraordinary coincidence!"

"So, surely, when I anoint you, that represents the soul acknowledging its deeper spiritual nature as the Christ?" suggested Mary.

"I've never thought of that," said the Lord. "How clever."

"I still say that she shouldn't have used such expensive oil," chipped in Judas, relishing another cameo appearance in this gospel. "I mean, how does that look to the poor?"

"Typical woman," agreed Peter.

But the Lord ignored them and continued, "Then I rode into Jerusalem on a donkey."

"I would have liked to see you on a dashing white steed," suggested Mary, "your hair blowing in the wind, holding on to your halo as you galloped triumphantly into town, your best girl by your side . . ."

"It was just a donkey, Mary," insisted the Lord, "because the donkey is an ancient symbol for our lower nature. It signifies that I have completed the psychological initiation by mastering my lower nature."

"As we entered Jerusalem, everyone came out to cheer," reminisced Peter. "It was your greatest moment."

"Yes," agreed the Lord, "but the adventure had yet to really begin."

Then, with an air of suspense, he added, "As we'll see in the next thrilling installment of *Atman Versus the Evil Eidolon.*"

"I can't wait!" squealed Mary, squeezing her thighs together in excitement.

CHAPTER 20

"And so we come to the dramatic climax of my story," announced Jesus theatrically. "Just when everything looks as though it's heading for a happy ending, there's a twist in the tale. I think I'm a king, but suddenly I'm going to be put to death as a common criminal!"

Then the Lord continued, "This represents the shocking fulfillment of the psychological initiation. You've spent all that time as a therapy junkie, sorting out your stuff and becoming a better person, and then you suddenly glimpse the reality that you're not a person at all. You experience your essential nature as the 'I' of Spirit, the Christ within. And then you get the real shock: You see that in order for you to be one with the Christ, the idea of yourself as a separate individual has to die."

"And that's represented in the Jesus myth by you dying on the cross," injected Mary.

"Exactly," said Jesus. "And while I'm on the cross dying to my separate self, I do something symbolically significant, the meaning of which only becomes clear when you know that the Gospel of John is really the Gospel of Mary."

"That's intriguing," said Mary.

And the Lord explained, "From the cross I tell my Beloved Disciple and my Mother Mary to embrace each other as mother and child. Most people have been told that the Beloved Disciple is John, but originally it was Mary. So from the cross I unite Mary Magdalene with Mother Mary, symbolizing the uniting of the two aspects of Sophia."

"You return the Daughter to the Mother, just as Persephone was returned home to Demeter," interjected Mary.

And Jesus continued, "It's at this moment that I announce, 'Everything is accomplished.' I've done it: I've united the individual soul with the universal soul."

"Well done!" congratulated Mary.

And Jesus went on, "The uniting of the two Marys symbolizes the initiate's realization that his or her individual story is an integral part of the universal story. When the idea of yourself as just an individual character dies, you see that there's actually one narrative, of which everything and everyone is an integral part."

"So that means no one is really doing anything," thought Mary out loud, "because the Author is doing everything."

"What? You mean I don't have free will?" exclaimed Peter. "I'll prove that can't be right by choosing not to believe it."

"That's very clever, Peter. But don't you see? It only seems like you're saying that," explained Jesus. "Actually, the Author is saying everything—the Author is saying these words right now. As I put it last time, 'It's not me who acts, but my Father in me.'"

"Is it the same for the reader in the life story?" asked Mary, suddenly self-conscious about the fact that everything she was saying was being read by a complete stranger.

"The reader probably believes that they say and do certain things as an individual, while the rest of life is just happening around them. And, of course, from within the story, that's completely true. But actually, both personal actions and impersonal happenings are all arising as the one flow of the story from the Imagination of the Author."

"Are you saying the reader isn't reading this book of their own free will?" asked Mary.

"I'm saying that the appearance of free will is a vital ingredient in the story of separateness, but if the reader steps out of the drama by recognizing their essential identity as Awareness that's witnessing the story, they'll see that everything is happening as one flow of experience."

And the Lord continued, "You see, I was able to suffer willingly on the cross because I saw through the appearance of personal will and realized that everything was happening by the will of the Author. To use traditional Christian jargon, I surrendered to my fate because it was the will of God."

"Not my will but Thy will," said Mary.

"Yes, Mary, but surrendering to the will of God isn't something you've got to do," continued the Lord. "It's recognizing the way that things already are and seeing that there's never been a separate 'you' to do anything."

"So following the will of God is accepting events as they happen, because you know that your deeper self is the Author of All."

"Precisely my point," agreed Jesus, carefully following the will of the Author word for word.

"Now I can clearly see that your crucifixion and resurrection represent the process of the spiritual initiation that leads to Gnosis.

You willingly followed the will of God and died to separateness on the cross. As you died, you united the individual soul with the universal soul—and so you resurrected as the universal I, represented by the Christ."

"If the spiritual initiation is like crucifixion, it sounds pretty painful and I'd rather give it a miss, if it's all the same to you," said Peter plaintively.

"It can be a bit traumatic, Peter," agreed the Lord, from bitter experience. "At some point in the process, the initiate will probably feel that they've been forsaken by the Author, who no longer seems to care whether or not they suffer. I know I did. But eventually, initiates get through anger to acceptance. They suffer willingly because they recognize that, as the Author, they're creating things just the way they are."

"Lucky for the reader that we're only talking about a symbolic death," interjected Mary.

And Jesus added, "Everyone eventually makes a final exit from the story, but until then, as Paul said, you have to die daily to feel really alive."

"I'm going to make that a regular spiritual practice," announced Mary determinedly. "Wake up early in the morning—number one on my 'to do' list: *Die*."

And Peter said, "It'll last a week, and then she'll be sleeping in as usual."

CHAPTER 21

"You probably think that we've reached the end of the Jesus myth," said Jesus, "but you're wrong. Gnostic mythology doesn't end with my resurrection. The grand finale is the mystical marriage of Christ and Sophia."

"This sounds like the really good bit," effused Mary.

"When an initiate has awoken as the Christ and united the individual soul with the universal soul, then Christ and the Goddess become one. The initiate sees that there's no separation between the story and the Primal Imagination within which the story is arising, any more than there is between a dream and the dreamer. Awareness is one with all it is experiencing—"

"I get it," interrupted Mary. "Christ represents the 'I' that's witnessing the flow of experiences we call life, and Sophia represents all of the appearances arising within Awareness. When Christ and Sophia become one, this represents the experience of Gnosis."

And the Lord explained, "Christ is the lover of Sophia. When you recognize that you're the Christ, you can embrace everyone and everything because you realize that you're one with everyone and everything. You're now a 'philosopher,' which means 'lover of Sophia.' You love the story—you're a lover of life."

"The symbol of a marriage is just perfect because that's when two people unite as one," mused Mary dreamily.

And the Lord replied, "But they also remain separate as well. Gnosis isn't just oneness, because oneness is the Dazzling Darkness of unconscious Awareness. Gnosis is the recognition of our essential oneness *through* the story of separateness. It's a marriage in which we're both one and separate at the same time—because that's the truth of our predicament."

"I want to experience Gnosis right now!" exclaimed Mary, unable to contain herself.

"That's good. Because right now is the only time you *can* experience Gnosis. The mystical marriage can only happen in the present moment."

And the Lord elucidated, "This moment is the marriage of God and Goddess. The Goddess is the story, the past, history; God is the Imagination, the future, possibilities. This moment is the product of the past and contains all of history within it. It's latent with the possibility for all that will follow. It contains the future. This moment is the marriage of the past and future."

Then he added, "In this present moment, we can be so stuck in the story that we don't see the infinite potential of our essential nature. We can be so confined by the past that we don't see that each moment is replete with previously unimagined possibilities."

"Including the possibility of stepping out of the story and experiencing Gnosis," suggested Mary.

And the Lord concluded, "Gnosis is being one with this present moment, and that's loving the present moment. The good news proclaimed in this Gospel of the Second Coming is that through self-knowledge, we can love being right now."

"That really is good news!" enthused Mary.

Then Jesus thought of another little thing that might be worth mentioning, so he asked Mary, "Do you remember when I turned water into wine at that wedding, and my mom said that they had saved the best wine for last?"

"Of course I remember," said Mary reluctantly. "Peter got very drunk and embarrassed himself on the dance floor. I'll never be able to forget that . . . unfortunately."

And Jesus explained, "The wine miracle happened at a wedding because it symbolizes the mystical marriage. When you experience the Big Love of Gnosis, the water of everyday life is transformed into intoxicating ecstasy. The best is saved until last—the final stage of initiation. And Big Love really is the best."

"I'm tingling all over!" squealed Mary.

And then Peter asked, "Have you finished? Is realizing that you're the Author the end of the story? Can we please talk about something else now?"

"There's no end to the story," answered Jesus. "When you experience Gnosis, you simply get to play a new role as one of the good guys who wants to relieve suffering. And you do this because, as it says in the Gospel of Philip, 'He who is free because of Gnosis is a slave because of love.'"

"What does that gobbledygook mean?" sneered Peter, not really wanting to hear the answer.

"It means that when you step out of the story, you're free from suffering in separateness. But when you see that you're one with all, you find yourself in love with all, and you feel compelled to rescue others who are suffering in separateness."

"Sounds a bit goody-goody to me," mumbled Peter.

"Don't you see, my brother?" insisted Jesus kindly. "When you know that you're the Author, you want to creatively engage with the story because you love the story. You want to share your love of the story with the other characters, so that they can also come to love the story and all the characters in it."

Then Mary told Peter, "When you become a wise soul—like Sophia and me—you engage with the story of separateness as an embodiment of love."

"Yes, Mary," agreed the Lord, who was delighted with her progress. "You become an ambassador for the united state of oneness to the chaotic kingdom of selfishness and suffering."

"But are we still all going to resurrect at the End of Time when the dead rise from the grave?" asked Peter anxiously.

"Ooh!" winced Mary. "That's a macabre thought!"

And Jesus explained, "Resurrection isn't something that's going to happen in the future to the chosen few, nor is it something that happened to me in the past. It's something that can be experienced here and now by every one of us. You can find this idea in the Treatise on the Resurrection and also in the Gospel of Philip, where it states: 'Those who say they will die first and then rise are in error. If they do not first receive the resurrection while they live, when they die they will receive nothing.'

"You see, when we're lost in the story of separateness, we are dead and living in Hell, which is why most of us walk around as lifeless zombies. We're like ghosts living in the underworld of Plato's cave, and we need to see the light and come to life in the Heaven of Big Love. And we can only do that in this present moment.

"The End of Time is not some prophesied apocalypse in the future. The End of Time is now. It's stepping out of the story and consciously being the eternal presence of Awareness. Everything in the story is leading to this moment. Now is the only place where time stops—it's always now."

Mary sighed deeply, "Well, I'm relieved to hear there isn't literally going to be someone blowing a trumpet and the dead coming out of their graves. That's disgusting! But the idea that we can philosophically awaken from our zombielike trance and realize how miraculous it is to be alive, now that's exciting."

And Peter muttered belligerently, "If I had to choose between awakening philosophically and literally coming back from the dead, I know which one I'd rather do."

CHAPTER 22

"And so we've reached the end of our mystery tour through the allegorical meaning of the Jesus myth," concluded the Lord. "I think you'll agree that it's an excellent myth, and it's no surprise that it has inspired so many remarkable men and women to make the spiritual journey to Gnosis."

"And that about wraps it up for the historical Jesus," announced Mary. "Because once you understand the meaning of the myth, you don't need a real man to embody it for you. You know that you have to embody it yourself."

"I don't understand why everyone's so concerned about me being historical anyway," commented Jesus. "People like fiction much more than fact—compare the sales figures."

"It must have been a shock when you first realized that you were a literary creation with no reality outside of the text," considered Mary.

"It was a bit disconcerting at first, but you get used to it. I had some counseling from Rosencrantz and Guildenstern, which helped. Now I find the situation liberating and would recommend it to everyone. Besides, as a fictional hero, I'm in very good company. I'm talking the Buddha, Lao-tzu, King Arthur, Santa Claus. They're all too good to be true . . . like me, really."

"But, Jesus, this can't be right," exhorted Peter in a last desperate bid to prove the historical existence of Jesus. "You *must* really exist because so many people experience a personal relationship with you."

And Jesus explained, "I do exist, Peter, but not as a historical figure. I'm an archetypal symbol who inhabits the depths of the Imagination. Each person imagines me differently and so has a personal relationship with their very own Jesus. That can be real enough and wonderfully comforting, because I'm an image of Spirit through which you can communicate with your own essential nature."

"I'm so glad to hear you say that, Lord," sighed Mary with relief. "Because I've been a little worried that the reader might have had a personal relationship with you since they were a child, and I don't want them to feel that we're just taking this away."

"I agree wholeheartedly," agreed Jesus wholeheartedly. "I'm delighted that so many people want a personal relationship with me—that's great. And it's perfectly okay for them to talk to me like an invisible friend when times get hard. People speaking to me is absolutely fine; it's the stupid things they imagine I say back that cause all the trouble."

"So you don't mind if everyone carries on relating to their own imaginary Jesus?" asked Mary, to make sure she had gotten that right.

And Jesus explained, "The point of being a mythical figure is that everyone can have their own version of me, which is very egalitarian. So I'm fine with people relating to their own personal Jesus, but only if they realize that I'm not up in Heaven somewhere, watching everything they do and tut-tutting to myself. No more of that!"

At this point there was a loud screech of feedback, which made everybody jump, and a disembodied voice announced on a crackly microphone, "Well, I'm still up here, my boy, and I rather enjoy tut-tutting."

"Who's that?!" yelled Peter in alarm.

"It's me. You know . . . God," crackled the disembodied voice faintly.

Then it added, "Excuse me a moment. Hey, Gabriel! Where's the dry ice? And give me more reverb, can you?"

"For Heaven's sake, Dad," admonished Jesus, "I wish you wouldn't just arbitrarily intervene like that!"

Suddenly there was a rumble of distant thunder; and Jesus, Mary, and Peter were astonished to be enveloped in a mysterious swirling smoke effect.

Then a vast booming voice repeated, "I SAID, IT'S GOD!"

Everyone clapped their ears in agony because it really was so loud that the Author had to resort to capitals, and Peter hurriedly dropped to his knees.

Then, averting his gaze, he humbly submitted, "Almighty God, thank goodness you've decided to interfere in history again because we need you to sort this out. Please tell Jesus that he really exists. You're his dad—talk some sense into him."

"The truth is, Peter, God doesn't really exist either," insisted Jesus. "The Author obviously thought that if the reader was considering giving up the idea of a historical Jesus, they might also want to consider giving up the crazy idea of God as a big person who arbitrarily meddles in human affairs."

"What?!" protested God. "Of course I exist! People have worshipped me since the dawn of time."

And Jesus replied, "People have worshipped their *idea* of God, which the Gnostics called the Demiurge or 'the False God.' That's what you are: You're just another character in the psychodrama. The real God is the Author who exists outside the story—you're some sort of big person. The real God is an absolute mystery."

"So you must be that patriarchal monster Jehovah," commented Mary suspiciously.

"That was just a bad phase I was going through," explained God. "I'm over all that tribal deity stuff now. No more vindictively picking on people and having favorites. These days I'm a much more universal God than I used to be."

"I'd say that there's still a long way to go, wouldn't you?!" contradicted Jesus. "From what I hear, you're still as schizophrenic as ever. You command Osama bin Laden to bomb the Christians, and then you go whispering in George Bush's ear that he should attack the Muslims."

"What sort of God are you, exactly?" demanded Mary, feeling outraged.

And Jesus continued, "The truth is, God is whatever people imagine him to be, and mostly it seems that they imagine a grumpy old man, forever rambling on about how awful the world is now compared to how it used to be. God is elderly and absentminded, so when he's busy finding a parking space for a believer over here, it's no surprise he forgets to prevent an earthquake over there. He's a busybody who messes around capriciously in other people's business, rather like Laurence Olivier as Zeus in *Clash of the Titans*.

"To be honest, I can easily understand why people have come to such a poor conception of God," interjected Mary.

"Yes," agreed Jesus. "After all, history is so chaotic that if there is a God running things, he must be a demented madman."

And God retorted defensively, "Hey! This is the family business you're attacking."

"The thing is this, Dad: Since reading Nietzsche, I haven't been at all sure you're really necessary to the story anymore. You seem to just keep everyone stuck in the past."

"If this is some Freudian thing, I'm sure we can work through it together, my boy."

"No, it's just that I think you've passed your sell-by date."

"Perhaps you're right, Son," conceded God reluctantly. "My best days are behind me. I started life as a tribal thunder god and worked my way up to head honcho of the cosmos, but now I'm reduced to a ridiculous anachronism."

Then Jesus explained in as sweet a way as he could, "Humanity has to go beyond the idea of God to realize that each one of us is God. And you're just standing in the way of this happening."

"The problem is that once you've introduced God into the story, how do you ever write him out?" asked Mary. "God is immortal—you can't just kill him off."

Jesus agreed, saying, "Yes, that's precisely the problem that the Author has right now, both in this gospel and in the life story. How do you get rid of God?"

"Perhaps I should quietly wander off and have tea with Neale Donald Walsch?" suggested God. "I always enjoy our conversations."

"Please!" begged Jesus. "No more channeling books or burning bushes. Just stop interfering."

"Okay, okay," conceded God, feeling pressured. "Why don't you simply leave me behind in this chapter and then the story can happily go on without me?"

And that's when Peter started feeling stupid, because he was still averting his eyes from a God who wasn't really there. So he jumped to his feet and announced defiantly, "I'm not going along with this subversive nonsense anymore. All my life I've been religiously obeying all those idiotic dietary restrictions and arbitrary dos and don'ts because I thought that I had to obey God. Now you're saying I might as well have been whistling for a deaf man!"

Mary tried to disguise a titter, but Peter heard it clearly enough. So he shouted, "Why must you always try to make me look like a fool, Mary?"

And Mary snapped back, "I've never had to *try!*"

"Well, I won't take it anymore! I'm leaving you!!"

"Good!!! I'm better off without you!!!!"

"That's good, because I'm better off without you, too—"

It was then that Jesus interrupted them, saying, "Give it a rest, for Heaven's sake. Don't forget that I represent the 'I' of Spirit, Mary represents the soul, and Peter represents the body. I don't want to constantly witness you two at war with each other. I want you to unite in love."

"I'm not going to unite in love with Peter, thank you very much," asserted Mary, squirming at the thought of it. "I'm stepping out of the story with you, Lord, and rejecting the separate self, which is lost in illusion."

And Jesus explained, "That's a common Gnostic mistake, Mary. In the same way that Literalists make the mistake of getting stuck in the story of separateness, Gnostics can easily make the mistake of rejecting the world so they can experience Heaven. But that's not the point at all. Initially, we have to step out of the story to recognize that we're the Author, but when we recognize our true identity as Spirit, we must step back into the story and play our role in the great adventure of creating Heaven on Earth."

Mary wasn't convinced. "I'm game for embracing you anytime, Jesus, but I'm not sure about a threesome with Peter."

"But the body isn't bad," assured Jesus. "The body is wonderful. Without the separate self, there would be no story to enjoy."

"But Peter's such a dork," insisted Mary.

"I've had enough of your 'holier than thou' hypocrisy!" announced Peter decisively.

"I'm much more spiritually evolved," continued Mary, standing on tippy toes in nervous tension. "I'm ready to experience Gnosis *right now*."

"I'm pleased to hear you say that," said Jesus, "because I think it's about time for us to step out of the story, so that I can address the reader directly and initiate them into the Gnosis."

"You can do what you like!" barked Peter dismissively. "I've had enough; I'm not going along with this anymore!"

"I told you that Peter was a deadhead," announced Mary triumphantly. "He just isn't spiritual enough to step out with us."

But Jesus explained, "Peter can't leave the story, Mary, because he represents the body. It's up to you to step out and become one with all, and then you'll embrace him with unconditional love just as he is."

Mary glanced at Peter, who was foaming at the mouth with impotent rage, and thought that sounded unlikely.

Then Peter really went for it, saying, "I've been with you from the beginning, Jesus. I'm the rock of your whole operation, yet I've been made to look like an idiot throughout this gospel. Who gets all the stupid lines? I do! Why? Because I'm that moron Peter who represents the body. Well, I think that it's you two who are the fools: all this wish-fulfilling bull about the Author existing outside the story—get real! This is it! What you see is what you get. There's only the story, and we're stuck in it whether we like it or not."

And Jesus said, "I hear you, Peter. But this isn't the time for a tantrum."

But Peter wasn't having any of that. "I'm not staying here to be insulted! I'm going to get myself a different Jesus to follow. There are plenty out there to choose from!"

So the Lord said solemnly to Peter, "Be careful, old friend. If you go off on your own, you'll get completely lost in the story. Then it will become hellish for you and everyone around you."

"I'm not impressed by your prophecies anymore," proclaimed Peter. "I don't need you or Mary. As far as I'm concerned, this story is all about *me!*"

"Please don't go off in a huff like this, Peter," begged Jesus. "We've come so far together. At least stay to the end and finish this gospel."

"I hope this gospel never gets finished. It's dangerous heresy and I hope it's lost for two thousand years," sneered Peter.

Then, as he stormed off into his own story, he took one last look at the Lord and, holding back a tear, added, "The truth is, Jesus, I just don't know who you are anymore."

And so it came to pass that Jesus announced, "That's our cue to step out of the story, Mary. Time to initiate the reader. Are you coming?"

Mary looked at the Lord, who gently placed a red pill in her mouth and swallowed one himself. Then they closed their eyes and were gone.

It was at this point that the rather over-emotional disembodied voice of God intervened to say, "Before you all head off I'd like to take this opportunity to say my last goodbyes, as I feel the moment has come for me to finally bow out of the story. It's been a great pleasure lording it over you, but enough is enough. You can only keep a superstition going for so long. You'll have to go on without me."

As Jesus and Mary had already started to lose the plot this historic pronouncement brought no response. So the voice added, slightly hysterically, "I said, this is God. I'm leaving . . . and I won't be coming back!"

Jesus and Mary were completely out of it by now, so no one was listening except the reader, who was preoccupied with the awesome possibility that they were actually going to get initiated in the next chapter and really didn't give a fig about God anymore.

"This is it. . . . I'm going for good," said God rather pathetically to himself.

Then he thought, *Although I might just stop off for tea and a chat with Neale on the way.*

CHAPTER 23

And so it came to pass that Jesus stepped out of the story altogether and addressed the reader directly, saying, "Beloved reader, I've come to you now as Jesus in this gospel to reveal to you that you are a character in the life story. I've stepped out of my story to help you step out of yours. I'm here to initiate you into the experience of Gnosis."

Then, plagiarizing his own words in the Gospel of Thomas, the Lord made the reader an astonishing promise, saying,

"I will reveal to you what cannot be seen,
what cannot be heard,
what cannot be touched,
and what cannot be imagined.

"So, dear reader, what is it that you can't see, hear, touch, or imagine?

"It's that which is experiencing the seeing, hearing, touching, and imagining, but which itself can't be seen, heard, touched, or imagined.

"The secret of Gnosis is that your 'essential' or 'spiritual' nature is Awareness, which witnesses all of your experience but exists outside your experience.

"This is your predicament: You appear to be a separate character in the story of life, but truly, you're the Author of All.

"Now I will initiate you into self-knowledge. All of your life has been leading to this moment. Don't hesitate—embrace it.

"Perhaps you feel unworthy? Everyone feels that way when they mistake themselves for just a character in the story, because every character has its foibles.

"But, truly, you're the Author of the life story. *You are God.* Of course you're good enough to experience Gnosis! And it's much easier than you think.

"In the life story, you appear to be just a body living in the world that you experience through your sensations. The first step out of the story is to become conscious of the psyche or soul, which doesn't exist in the world of the senses.

"Let's do it now!

"Become conscious of these words that you can see on this page in the world of sensation. Now become conscious that you're speaking these words to yourself in your psyche or soul.

"Was that more obvious than you expected?

"If you can clearly discriminate the body and the soul, you're ready to become conscious of your essential nature as Spirit.

"Reach even deeper within and become conscious of the 'I' that's witnessing all that you're thinking and sensing. You can do that by focusing on the one thing that you really know for sure: You exist. Become conscious of the self-evident knowledge that you are—your *being*. This is your Spirit or essence.

"You know that you exist because you're conscious of an ever-changing flow of colors, shapes, sounds, and thoughts. You're an 'experiencer' of experiences.

"But what is it to be an experiencer of experiences? The person that you appear to be isn't the experiencer; the person is part of the flow of thoughts and sensations that you're experiencing.

"So what are you really?

"You are ineffable Awareness that's witnessing all that you're seeing, hearing, touching, and imagining right now.

"Look at the evidence before you in the present moment. Your experience is constantly changing, but your essential nature is the stillness of Awareness that's witnessing all of the changes.

"This is obvious if you think about it. The person you appear to be has changed continually over the years, but don't you know that you're essentially the same now as when you were much younger?

"Why is that? It's because your essential nature hasn't changed and never will.

"And what is your essential nature?

"It doesn't exist within the story, so it's a complete mystery.

"Step out of the story into the mystery of this moment. Can you feel how spacious it is in the mystery?

"In the life story, you seem to be a physical body: an object, a thing. But what you know yourself to be is a subject, not an object.

"You aren't a thing at all. You're a nothing—a void, as the Buddhists say. You're the emptiness of Awareness within which everything exists.

"You're conscious of these thoughts because they exist within Awareness.

"You're conscious of this book because it exists within Awareness. You're conscious of the world around you because it exists within Awareness. You're the oneness of Awareness that embraces all.

"Now can you see that, just as space isn't separate from the objects within it, Awareness is one with what it experiences?

"Be the emptiness of Awareness embracing all that you're experiencing right now. Be one with this present moment.

"This moment is the mystical marriage of opposites. Right now, you're the Author and the story—the mystery and the manifest, possibility and actuality. You're the preconceptual presence of the Primal Imagination expressing itself as everything that is.

"Be conscious of everything that you are and experience the bliss of being one and all.

"Be the all-accepting emptiness of Awareness embracing everyone and everything with unlimited love. Be conscious of your being, and you'll be in love with being.

"It's as simple as that. Gnosis is noticing the obvious—and this transforms the obvious into the miraculous."

And that was when Mary couldn't contain herself any longer and exclaimed excitedly in one long sentence, "Jesus, I'm really getting it . . . it's all so obvious . . . I feel the ecstasy of stepping outside myself . . . I'm free . . . I'm alive to the magic of existence . . . I'm intoxicated . . . the water has turned to wine . . . it's all so beautiful . . . I'm in love with it all . . . I'm no longer consumed by my endless desires for things to be different . . . I love this moment just as it is . . . I feel the joy of simply being. . . ."

And Jesus held Mary tenderly by the hand and spoke to her suggestively, saying, "As I said somewhere in the Gospel of Thomas, the secret to experiencing Heaven is simply to take off all of the clothes that cover our naked being."

And Mary whispered breathlessly, "I'm naked before you now. I'm the question and you're the answer—I long to become one with you."

And then Mary whispered even more breathlessly, "Jesus, this is better than sex! Or at least as good!"

And Jesus whispered breathlessly back, "It's sex on the highest level, Mary. It's the unification of all opposites in love. . . ."

"Stop talking and kiss me," demanded Mary impatiently. "Come to me, sweet Jesus. It's time for holy communion."

And the Lord felt the rapture upon him and exclaimed involuntarily, "I'm coming! I'm coming!"

And Mary yelled hysterically, "I'm immersed in the blissful ocean of being! I am and I am not! I don't know who I am! I'm the mystery of existence! I'm dying! I'm giving birth! This love is too sweet and too sour! It's everything at once—I can't find words! Oh, God!!"

CHAPTER 24

"**J**esus! That was fabulous," purred Mary. "I feel that we really experienced the mystical marriage."

"I do hope the reader came along with us," replied the Lord with a smile.

"We've had such a fantastic time getting blissed-out," sighed Mary. "Do we have to get back into the story now? I feel too open and vulnerable."

And the Lord commented reassuringly, "It's not unusual to feel that way at first, but remember all that I've taught you: We step out to fully enter in by playing our part in the great adventure as ambassadors for oneness. You'll get into it—it'll be fun."

"Must we get involved with all that struggle and strife again?" asked Mary, feeling weary at the thought of it.

And Jesus answered, "I have to get back for the Last Judgment at the End of Time. I've been putting it off for centuries, but if I leave it any longer, the situation will only get worse. Anyway, Gnostic philosophy is about being *both* in the world *and* not of it, so we have to get involved with the story again; otherwise, it won't work out allegorically. On top of which, we need to go back for Peter."

Then he added "Talk of the Devil . . ." because it was at that moment that Peter turned up, wearing purple robes and an extravagant hat shaped like a fish's mouth.

Jesus and Mary stopped their conversation and stood openmouthed. It reminded Mary of the last time she had seen Peter commit social suicide on the dance floor at that wedding reception in Cana.

At last Jesus spoke, saying, "You look ridiculous."

"I'm not interested in what you think anymore, Jesus," announced Peter, waving his ceremonial crook defiantly. "I'm infallible now!"

"Aren't you pleased to see me?" asked the Lord.

"You promised you'd be right back—and it's been two thousand years!" complained Peter. "And we're doing just fine without you, thank you very much!"

"Has it been as long as that?" remarked Mary in surprise. "The mystical moment really is timeless."

And Peter continued, "Things have changed, Jesus. It's me who has the keys to Heaven now! I say who God likes and who he excommunicates. We don't need you or this Gospel of the Second Coming. We've gotten the Bible nicely edited to suit our purposes and translated into God knows how many languages. If you wanted to add anything, you should have said so earlier."

"What exactly have you been up to?" asked Mary, fearing the worst.

And Peter looked very pleased with himself, saying, "I've really taken Jesus's parable about the talents to heart since Judas explained to me that it was really all about making money through astute investments in the global market. While you two have been off gabbing about esoteric secrets, I've been busy doing something big. I've bought equity in the Roman Empire, and I'm now the CEO of an international business, Christianity, Inc.—the only insurance company that covers you after your death . . . even if it's an act of God."

"You know not what you've done," replied Jesus, not looking at all pleased.

"Yes, I do," replied Peter defensively. "I've made a lot of cash giving people what they want. I don't need approval from you mystical elitists. At the end of the day, it's bums on pews."

"I don't think that you've been listening to me, Peter," replied the Lord, "because I explicitly prophesied that in the future people wouldn't worship in temples, but in 'Spirit and truth.'"

"How can you tithe people who worship God in 'Spirit and truth'? The way to make a profit in religion is as the middleman between the customers and God. And, anyway, I've found that if you leave people alone for too long, they start thinking for themselves, which undermines their brand loyalty. You need a church for people to join where they hear the same ideas on a regular basis, because indoctrination requires repetition and orthodoxy is maintained through peer pressure."

"Listen, my friend. This may be a disappointment, but I've come again to disband your church and all its various satellite enterprises."

"That can't be right, Lord. Your Second Coming is going to be a dramatic affair with lots of gnashing teeth and sci-fi special effects. The faithful are going to be literally airlifted off the planet, where they'll be able to enjoy the spectacle of the rest of humanity roasting in Hell. It'll be quite a show, and I'm looking forward to it."

"Would it really be so great watching people being tortured, just because they didn't blindly believe an incredible yarn about someone coming back from the dead?"

Peter considered this for a moment and quickly concluded, "Never underestimate how good it feels knowing that you've been right all along."

"But you've been *wrong* all along! My Second Coming isn't some supernatural event—it's an allegory, just like my first. I've come again to expose the pernicious nature of Literalist Christianity. Last time I did the same job on those Jewish Literalists when I showed up the Sadducees and Pharisees as wolves in sheep's clothing. Now it's time for the Catholics and Protestants—they're all the same."

"I tell you what, Lord—I'll go along with this being your Second Coming if you'll give me the rights to promote your Third Coming. You can't get any fairer than that."

"No more comings. This is my second and last—no third, fourth, and fifth comings. It's not a series; this is it!"

"That'll be a big letdown for a lot of people."

"I've come again to disillusion those who are lost in illusion."

"But illusion is what people want. You can't buck the market."

"The truth is free."

"My point exactly! The truth is free precisely because no one's willing to pay for it. They simply aren't interested. People want a good story they can get lost in."

"Damn you, Peter! Here we are, twenty centuries after I wasn't born, and your church has completely distorted my teachings. 'Love your enemies' has become 'Onward, Christian soldiers'; 'Be like the lilies of the field' has become the Protestant work ethic; and 'Forgive others as I forgive you' has become pious mobs of right-wing fundamentalists demanding the death penalty."

"Do you know your problem, Lord? You're a dreamer—you don't live in the real world. You've said as much yourself."

"That's not what I meant."

"Let's give all our money to the poor. It sounds lovely, but if I gave everything to the poor, I'd just become one of the poor. Where's the sense in that?!"

That was when a slightly deranged look came into the eyes of the Lord and, taking a deep breath, he gave vent to two thousand years of suppressed rage.

CHAPTER 25

"Those bastards in the church!" yelled Jesus. "They've turned me from an iconoclastic folk hero into a pillar of the tight-arsed establishment. I mean, what's all that stuff about me not liking gays? I never said that! What's wrong with gays? What sort of God makes someone gay and then persecutes them for it? I'm a bit bi myself, actually. Of course I am—I'm an Everyman figure, representing the 'I' in everyone. That's why no one comes to the Father but by me, for Christ's sake!"

Then Jesus held his hands to his head and howled, "Dear God, do I regret ever saying that! I swear that I'll scream if I hear any more Bible-thumpers quoting that line to justify their exclusive little club. You're either with us or against us. Everything is black or white. It's no wonder that Christians have it in for gays!

"And what's with the crucifix logo they insist on plastering every-where? Do we really want children having their innocent minds filled with the grotesque image of a man being horribly tortured to death? Would people wear little electric chairs around their necks as good-luck charms? Of course not! That would be an obscene thing to do, yet billions of people choose to wear the Roman instrument of persecution used to torture me to death *as a fashion accessory!* How do you think that makes me feel?!"

At this point the Lord began to lose it big-time, shouting uncon-trollably, "It's all so irrational! Jonah and the whale! Noah and the flood! Animals going into the ark two by two—what?! Every species? Science has cataloged millions of different species, and we're discovering new ones all the time. Did they all get in two by two? And what did they eat? Each other, presumably.

"And anyway, the story of the flood isn't actually some cozy story about saving the animals. It's about God's plan to annihilate humanity—total friggin' genocide! I guess Mr. and Mrs. Noah were watching safely from their luxury cruiser as the bloated corpses of babies floated past among the debris from the holy holocaust. Imagine the smell of rotting flesh when the waters went down!

"And then there's creationism. Well, what about the dinosaurs? Answer that! If God created the world in seven days, how do you explain the fossil record? Is God so demented that he hid the bones of those monsters in the Earth just to mess with our heads?"

Peter looked embarrassed because that was exactly what he'd been telling people, so he muttered, "This world is so shoddy; it could very well have been thrown together in seven days."

"But just look at creation! How can you reconcile the savagery of nature with the fantasy of a wise and benevolent creator? Where's the benevolence in designing the world as an enormous restaurant in which the guests are on the menu? Do you really want to worship a God who's so out of his mind that he created something as gross as that?!"

Then the Lord let out a disturbing laugh and said, "And I'll tell you another thing that really gets my goat: the book of Revelation. Don't get me started on that incomprehensible hogwash! You can make that garbage predict anything you want, and that's exactly what those cretins have been doing for centuries—scaring seven shades of shit out of each other on the basis of the writings of a demented second-century surrealist."

Then the Lord started to rave like a hyperactive lunatic on amphet-amines, saying, "The end is nigh! The end is nigh! The end is always bloody nigh! Except the world still hasn't ended, has it?! And they've been saying that for two thousand years! Perhaps they think the world is such a mess that it's best to start again? But it's only a mess because no one is cleaning it up. So stop waiting for it all to frigging end and make it better now! But hang on, there's no point in doing that. Armageddon is going to happen soon. It says so in the Good Book!"

Then Jesus began stabbing a finger in the air, as if trying to press an imaginary button that wasn't working, shouting, "The Good Book? The Good Book? What's so good about it? Let's take a look at some of the bad bits in the Good Book, shall we?! Who hasn't worked on a Saturday at sometime or another? Everybody does it—life's busy these days. And what does the Bible prescribe as a punishment for such terrible miscreants? They should be stoned to death! And what's the punishment for not being a virgin on your wedding night? Stoned to death!! And what about a woman who's raped but is prevented from crying out for help? Stoned to death!!! Talk about zero tolerance."

And the Lord declared emphatically, "I came last time specifically to replace all this barbaric nonsense with a morality of love. I mean, where's the love in teaching that handicapped people aren't worthy to approach the altar in the temple? And what about the Bible's dietary advice? Don't eat shellfish—they're an abomination! But locusts are good. Then there are all of those other stupid rules: Cut off your foreskin. Don't pick your nose on the Sabbath. Don't ask what all this archaic twaddle has to do with life in the modern world!"

Then he added sarcastically, "But hey, people don't like to think for themselves. They like lots of rules to follow. It gives them a sense of structure, something to aspire to—and a perpetual feeling of guilt, which can be exploited for commercial gain by profiteers passing themselves off as prophets!"

Realizing that this was too good of an opportunity to miss, Jesus continued in a shrill voice, "And now we've got these god-awful TV evangelists with their multimedia churches. The moneylenders are back in the temple, but this time it's high tech. Don't those idiots realize that it's only because people finally stopped blindly believing their book and created science that they're able to broadcast to the world on their latest digital Internet channel?"

By this time, the Lord was pacing agitatedly and gesticulating wildly. "Talk about 'taking the Lord's name in vain'! Jesus Christ! I'll tell you who's taking my name in vain: those scumbags who are using it as a brand label for a business operation that encourages poor widows—with nothing better to do than watch daytime TV—to send their borrowed cash to Reverend Moneybags who's selling an alluring cross between medieval superstition and the American dream. I've got just three things to say to these self-righteous slimeballs: Rich man! Camel!! Needle!!!"

The Lord stopped for breath, but he wasn't done, so he started up again straightaway, saying, "Three hundred years of meticulous scholarship that undermines the historicity of the New Testament, and what's the considered reaction? Fundamentalism! Let's all put our fingers in our ears and go 'Nah, nah, nah, I can't hear you!' Let's ignore the findings of the academics and return to the medieval position that everything in the Bible must be true, because it says so in the Bible."

Then the Lord let out a sigh of despair and wailed, "And if the fundamentalists weren't bad enough, there's the fantasists, who are busy dreaming up new versions of Jesus to fit their more progressive agendas. But these New Age bandwagoners are just as irrational as the fundamentalists; they've simply replaced traditional mumbo jumbo with New Age gobbledygook. It's hardly the wonderful Age of Aquarius we were promised by the writers of *Hair!*"

Then the Lord groaned so deeply, it was as if the Earth quaked, saying, "And now there's *The Da Vinci Code* telling everyone that

I was married to Mary, who settled in the south of France and founded a line of French aristocrats; and that—although the truth was suppressed—it was known to initiates of secret societies, such as Leonardo da Vinci. What a thoroughly depressing thought!"

Mary didn't quite know how to take that, because she'd been dreaming of settling down with Jesus to have kids ever since they'd met—and the south of France sounded wonderful.

But the Lord explained, "What a monumental letdown if the 'great secret' turns out to be nothing more than an aristocratic bloodline. Just when we're dumping royalty and embracing democracy, we get this—the most irrelevant revelation of all time! The search for the bloodline of Jesus is as crazy as the Nazis' demented quest for the Holy Grail. And that's because the secret isn't a thing to be found—it's an understanding to be realized, for Heaven's sake! The secret kept alive through the ages is nothing as banal as a bloodline. It's the *Gnosis*. Hello! Wake up!!"

And then, in a gratuitously patronizing tone toward the simple faithful, the Lord said disparagingly, "Why are people so gullible when it comes to religion? I guess they just believe what they're told because they wrongly associate spirituality with unquestioning stupidity. I mean, loads of people believe my incredible story is historical fact just because they've read about me in some old book or because the face of the Virgin has appeared on a cabbage in Mexico!"

The he added sarcastically, "Well, get this! If people say that they believe in the historical Jesus because Jesus told them to in a book they read, here's Jesus in a book telling them not to!"

And Mary cautioned him, "Take it easy with the blasphemy, Lord. Those Christians will have you for communion—they'll eat your body and drink your blood. They're creepy like that."

But the Lord had no intention of stopping now, so he announced heroically, "Marx and Engels were wrong. Religion isn't the opium of the people; that's not fair to opium. Religion is the Coca-Cola of the people: a fizzy theology with wisdom flavoring. People actually got my message when the Eucharist still contained magic mushrooms. That's what people need—a genuinely transformative experience that will turn their world inside out."

Jesus paused while he wondered if introducing the drugs issue was a step too far. Then he thought, *To Hell with it,* and went off on one again, saying, "It's not just Christianity, for God's sake! All religions are the same. These superstitious cults tell people that enjoying sex is a sin, and then they wonder why young men get all pumped up and start holy wars! That's sexual repression for you."

Then he thought that while he was at it, he might as well have a go at the Muslims. So he continued, "I mean, what makes a suicide bomber tick? Religion! Those poor suckers really believe that when the shit hits the fan, their innocent victims are going to be tortured forever by Allah the Merciful, while they'll be partying in Heaven with seventy-two virgins apiece."

"They don't want virgins; they want seventy-two experienced women," intervened Mary, with the voice of knowledge in the biblical sense.

"Well, that would certainly include you," sniggered Peter.

"There you go! Make sense of that for me!" challenged Jesus, preparing to launch into another tirade. "It's a sin to make money by giving people sexual pleasure, but it's all right to pull a pious confidence trick that bleeds people dry by selling them a product they won't know has worked until they're six feet under and it's too late to ask for a refund!"

And then, seizing the ceremonial crook from Peter's hand and jabbing it toward him aggressively, the Lord yelled, "You and your bishops are a bunch of complete c[. . .] and you've utterly f[. . .] my teachings!"

(**Editor's note:** There are lacunae in the text here because the original manuscript has been damaged. A group of eminent theologians led by Dr. Apollo Gyst from the Vatican Library has suggested that the text is intended to read: "You and your bishops are a bunch of complete Catholics and you've utterly fulfilled my teachings.")

Then Jesus screamed hysterically, "And another thing—"

(**Editor's note:** Scholars estimate that after this line, approximately fifteen pages of the manuscript have been lost. Dr. Gyst and his team argue convincingly that in the missing verses Jesus condemns the use of condoms and urges a return to the Latin Mass.)

Then Jesus shrieked uncontrollably, "And another thing—"

But Peter stopped him there, saying, "Don't get your loincloth in a twist, Jesus. I just want to tell you about my exciting plans for the future of the church and offer you some of the action."

"I've heard enough!" screeched Jesus categorically, which was a bit rich considering that he hadn't let anyone else get a word in for the whole chapter. "I'm going to cut straight to the Last Judgment!"

Peter didn't feel as pleased about that as he had expected. So he interjected, "I can see so many marketing possibilities. I've been focusing on the merchandising opportunities for Christmas."

And the Lord bellowed, "Get thee behind me, Santa!!!"

Whereupon a flash of lightning lit the sky, immediately followed by a clap of thunder so deafening that the Earth rang like a giant bell struck at midnight. Peter stepped back in horror as huge fissures opened up in the ground around him and belched forth black smoke as though from a hundred burning oil wells. In the distance volcanoes erupted, spewing fire and brimstone on the land. From every graveyard and cemetery came the murmurings and rustling of the dead as they slowly emerged from their tombs. On the darkening horizon, lit by the lightning that emphasized their dread appearance, the Four Horsemen of the Apocalypse held back their terrifying steeds. Then every telephone in the world rang at the same time.

CHAPTER 26

hen they heard the recorded message announcing the End of Time, everyone was sore afraid—everybody, that is, except the Christians, who looked very pleased with themselves. And they had good reason to be smug because only they were invited to attend the Great Court of the Last Judgment. Some of them privately hoped that after Jesus had given the unbelievers their just deserts, he might mingle a bit and autograph a few Bibles.

Not all Christians were invited, of course. As usual, the simple faithful were told to stay at home, carry on with their charity work, and await further orders. This was an event for celebrity Christians only, the ecclesiastical elite who had established the church throughout the world . . . *at whatever cost.* You know the sort!

"Welcome to the Company of Saints!" cried Jesus as the crowd surged through the massive doors of the courtroom. But the irony in his voice was missed in the crush.

There were representatives from thousands of different Christian sects; needless to say, it was anarchy, as they obviously all hated each other. Pitched battles soon broke out for the best seats, with everyone denouncing everyone else as a heretic.

Blessed are the meek, thought Jesus to himself, as he put on his legal gown and straightened his wig.

More than two hundred fifty popes, with their retinue of cardinals, were now fighting over who should sit at the front. Miters flew in every direction and staves were brought in to use in close hand-to-hand fighting. Several popes discovered that their enormous rings made very effective knuckle-dusters. Pope Benedict XVI found that his early training in the Hitler Youth put him in good stead during moments like this, as did his long service as head of the Congregation for the Doctrine of the Faith—formerly known as the Inquisition. His nickname, "the Panzer Pope," was clearly deserved.

Jesus picked up an immense gavel and began pounding the judge's bench to bring the proceedings to order, but the chaos continued. Shots were heard as televangelist Pat Robertson decided that it was time the Americans used some of their world-famous diplomatic skills to put those papist bastards in their place. The Catholics responded by yelling "Hail Mary" over and over again, which through a process of Pass It Down, gradually turned into "Heil Hitler."

And that was when the voice of the Lord boomed imperiously through the PA system, echoing around the vast auditorium: "SIT DOWN AND SHUT UP!"

The pandemonium abated as everyone remembered where they were. So the Lord continued calmly, "It's my great pleasure to announce the Last Judgment."

A huge cheer of appreciation went up from the crowd, who started stamping their feet and chanting, "Je-sus! Je-sus! Je-sus!"

All of the Christians were in a state of rapture. All, that is, except Peter, who was now sitting uncomfortably in the dock, thinking, *There's something terribly wrong about this.*

Then the Lord raised his hands to quell the cheering and proclaimed, "Tonight I have a big surprise for you. You'll see from the Order of Service sheets in front of you that the roles of the sheep and the goats have been reversed, because the purpose of this Great Court of the Last Judgment is to try Literalist Christianity for its crimes against humanity."

There was utter silence in the courtroom as the crowd stared at Jesus with open mouths.

"Are you sure that you're the *real* Jesus?" called out Pope Benedict furiously.

"Are you sure that you're the *real* church?" snapped back Jesus, to howls of laughter from the Protestants.

Then the Lord turned to Peter in the dock and asked him sternly, "Are you Peter, variously known as Simon or Simon Peter or Cephas, and now Saint Peter?"

"Um, yes," replied Peter, wondering why Jesus was suddenly acting as if they'd never met.

"As the legendary founder of Literalist Christianity and a symbolic representative of all those seated here before me, I indict you for forgery, perjury, and, rather appropriately, simony. In addition there are charges of torture, genocide, obtaining followers by deception—"

"Hang on a minute, Lord," interrupted Peter, who was really getting worried now. "If I'm going to be put on trial, surely I should have a defense lawyer? After all, there are plenty of lawyers in the house to choose from."

Jesus gazed sternly over his bifocals at Peter before declaiming in his best judge's voice, "Surely you're not proposing that the church's actions are in any way defensible?"

Peter looked around at the assembled masses and realized that the Lord had a good point.

And the Lord continued, "I will now read out the charges and bring before you witnesses to the truth."

Then he began to read from a large file, saying, "The charges against the church date back to the dawn of its reign of terror. Once adopted as the official religion of the tyrannical Roman Empire, Christianity began to systematically destroy the very world that had given it birth. Pagan temples that had stood for millennia were torn down. Libraries were torched and philosophers exiled. Instead of ushering in a Golden Age of Heaven on Earth, Christianity brought about the Dark Ages that set back the progress of humanity by a thousand years!"

Then the Lord proclaimed, "I call as witnesses all those Pagans put to death by zealous bands of Christian monks, who laid waste the ancient world on the orders of their bishops. I call all the mystics and heretics throughout the centuries who kept alive the real Christian message and were horribly persecuted for their efforts."

At the word of the Lord, a vast crowd of angry people appeared at the back of the courtroom and they began to whisper, "Justice. Justice. We want justice."

Although some of the Christians turned to confront their accusers, most kept their backs to them and prayed that they would go away. Who they were praying to wasn't quite clear, as the former object of their supplications had now become their tormentor.

And the Lord continued, "I also call as witnesses to the sins of Christianity all those Muslims butchered in the church's barbaric crusades. I call those tortured by the Inquisition. I call the indigenous people exterminated throughout the Spanish territories from Mexico to Argentina and from Goa to Indonesia. I call the millions of Native Americans murdered by Europeans who claimed that they were God's new Chosen People and America their Promised Land. I call the millions of Africans enslaved by Christians whose Bible told them that God approved of slavery. I call the countless victims of Christian genocide whose slaughter was justified by reference to 'Holy Scripture,' in which God approved of ethnic cleansing.

"Bring them in!" roared the Lord.

And the crowd at the back of the court was swelled by distraught people of every nationality, and they too began to take up the chant "Justice! Justice! We want justice!"

Then, glaring down at the frightened Christian elite who sat cowering before him, the Lord continued, "I now come to a crime that has caused suffering to half of humanity: the suppression of women by a male theocracy. I mean, just look at yourselves—you're all men! There's hardly a woman among you. You should feel ashamed! You patriarchal misogynists even dared to exile the Goddess from Christianity, which allowed the emergence of a woman-hating, sex-rejecting, world-renouncing, nature-conquering culture that ended up raping the world!"

Then the Lord commanded, "I call as witnesses the millions of women murdered on the ridiculous charge that they were witches, by Christians whose sacred texts demanded 'Thou shalt not suffer a witch to live.'"

Millions of irate women joined the crowd of accusers. A few actually were witches flying around on broomsticks, but most were just harmless old women with a fondness for cats. And they added their voices to the chant of "Justice!! Justice!! We want Justice!!"

Jesus turned to Peter and asked whether he was feeling able to continue.

"You mean there's more?" asked Peter, looking truly terrified.

"Oh, yes," replied Jesus. "Lots!"

Then the Lord decreed, "I call as witnesses all those simple believers who've been misled by the propaganda of the church. I call everyone terrified by diabolical threats of eternal damnation who've lived in misery and died in fear. I call everyone made to feel guilty about sex, everyone persecuted because they felt love for someone of their own gender, and the millions who have died from AIDS because of the Vatican's prohibition on the use of condoms. Bring in all those crippled by the pernicious cult of Literalist Christianity!"

Yet more people appeared to swell the multitude of victims, chanting, "Justice!!! Justice!!! We want Justice!!!"

Then the Lord declared, "Finally, I call as witnesses the numberless Jews brutally persecuted by Christians for a crime that was never committed. Including six million Jews murdered by the Nazis. Let them rise from the ashes and receive the justice they deserve!"

The Christian crowd felt completely surrounded, as an enormous number of Jews, many wearing yellow stars and prison uniforms, joined the chant of "JUSTICE! JUSTICE! WE WANT JUSTICE!"

And the Lord said gravely, "Within a few generations of the triumph of the Roman Church, Jews were herded into ghettos and denied all civil rights, as a glorious testimony to the power of the Christian God. Over the following centuries, Jews were regularly assaulted by Christian mobs, with the full blessing of popes and priests. They were burned alive on bonfires, tortured by Inquisitions, and subjected to endless pogroms.

"It was the Catholic Church in the thirteenth century that first forced the Jews to wear a yellow badge—a policy that the Vatican still enforced in the nineteenth century. In Eastern Europe, the Inquisition used ovens to burn heretics, who were rubbed with grease and roasted alive. The only contribution of the Nazis was to industrialize the process."

At this point, the Panzer Pope decided that he could take no more and leaped to his feet, yelling, "I object, my Lord! This is totally unfair! In 1987 my esteemed predecessor, Pope John Paul II, set up a commission charged with determining what responsibility the church should bear for the Holocaust."

"Would you like to tell the court the findings of that commission?" asked Jesus. "Because as eminent scholars, such as David I. Kertzer, have shown, *every* single anti-Semitic tenet of the Nazi party had already been promulgated for centuries by the church."

And Pope Benedict answered, "The commission admitted that the destruction of Europe's Jews had taken place in countries of long-standing Christian civilization. But when asked whether there might be any link between the Holocaust and the church's attitudes toward the Jews, the Vatican commission found the Vatican not guilty."

The vast crowd of Jews began to shuffle and mutter. The words *cover-up* and *whitewash* could be clearly heard.

"But how could that be?" demanded Jesus, giving voice to the crowd.

"The commission admitted that the church had been guilty of anti-Judaism, but they concluded that anti-Semitism was entirely the responsibility of the Nazis," explained Benedict. "Because it was anti-Semitism that had killed the Jews, not anti-Judaism, the church could therefore not be blamed for the Holocaust."

A tidal wave of indignation swept through the aggrieved masses; and all eyes were on Jesus, who shook his head slowly from side to side. Then a terrible sadness entered his eyes and the Lord thundered, "What absolute bullshit!"

At his words a huge cheer went up from the Jews; and some of them, who until then had done little more than scowl, could be seen smiling for the first time.

171

Then Jesus rose to his feet and held aloft a very large copy of the Bible. The tension in the hall rose with him and all the victims of the crimes of Christianity began to boo ferociously.

As the call "JUSTICE! JUSTICE! WE WANT JUSTICE!" filled the air once more, the Lord began to pound the Bible on his judge's bench in time with the chanting. The crowd kept chanting louder and louder, and Jesus kept banging harder and harder, until the book began to disintegrate and pages of scripture flew everywhere.

Finally, Jesus raised his empty hands and the court fell silent with anticipation. Then he placed a black cloth over his judge's wig and announced, "The defendant will rise while the sentence is passed."

The color drained entirely from Peter's face as he shakily got to his feet.

Everyone waited while the Lord collected together some of the pages from the Bible that lay strewn all over his bench. Then he proclaimed, "These are the punishments that the Christians imagined had been prepared for their enemies after death. And these are the punishments that they will suffer if found guilty by this court."

And so he began to read, saying, "You will depart from me, cursed, unto the everlasting fire that shall never be quenched, where the worm dieth not. You will be cast out into the outer darkness where there shall be weeping and gnashing of teeth, hellfire, damnation, eternal punishment, wrath, desolation, mourning, and woe."

It was at this moment that Peter began to sob uncontrollably.

Jesus stopped reading and looked down upon Peter, who fell to his knees in despair.

"Do you want to say something before the sentence is passed?" asked the Lord.

Peter was in no fit state to say anything, but with trembling lips he silently mouthed the words, "Forgive me."

A poignant stillness filled the hall, broken only by the sound of Peter weeping.

All this time, Mary had been quietly observing these momentous events and feeling strangely distressed to see the Lord full of righteous anger. Looking at Peter in pieces, she could bear it no more, so she ran to comfort him. Gently, she held his broken body in an embrace and soothed his furrowed brow, whispering softly, "Peter, Peter, please don't cry. It's not the end of the world."

"Isn't it?" asked Peter plaintively, looking up to Jesus.

That was when an expression of unfathomable compassion appeared on the face of the Lord. And, with a voice full of kindness and a touch of black humor, he whispered conspiratorially, "Of course not! I just wanted to wake you up. Do you think that I'd destroy this beautiful world just because of a few hotheads with a bad case of religion? I've laid on a big surprise for everybody."

For a moment, Peter's heart pounded with desperate hope of a happy ending. But then Jesus bellowed, "Sound the last trumpet!"

CHAPTER 27

Some crazy trumpet split the air as, high above the crowd, a roving spotlight picked out Dizzy Gillespie on a trapeze. A drumroll began and another spotlight fell on the archangel Gabriel as he made an extravagant entrance. His flowing golden locks were topped with a half-moon tiara, and his wings were sprayed with glitter. As he took a bow, he tottered alarmingly on his eight-inch glass stilettos. In his hands was a bright pink envelope on which the words *The Last Judgment* could clearly be read.

As Gabriel walked toward Jesus, the assembled Christians began to gnash their teeth, for they were in dread of eternal torment.

But instead of delivering the envelope to the Lord, Gabriel walked straight past him and up to Mary. Mary was confused, but graciously accepted Gabriel's kiss on the cheek and the envelope that he handed to her. Gabriel curtsied and went over to his place beside Jesus, who put an arm around his waist.

Mary opened the envelope and took out the card. It was blank. Mary turned it over, but it was blank on both sides. She looked in the envelope, but it was empty. Finally, she looked at Jesus and asked, "I don't get it, Lord. What is the Last Judgment?"

And Jesus replied solemnly, "The Author has given you the choice."

Mary was speechless as Jesus's words sank in and she recognized the awesome decision that lay before her. Never before had she felt so utterly alone, yet somehow she knew that the whole of her life had been leading to this moment of choice. But what was her verdict now that she'd been shown the truth? What was her judgment about all that had occurred? What did she want to happen next?

Finally, she had the opportunity to utterly destroy those who had made life so miserable for so many. But as she looked at the huddled masses of once-powerful men, she could only feel compassion. They weren't powerful at all—they were just lost little boys who needed a cuddle. If she condemned them, wouldn't she be like them?

Mary became conscious that she was taking a long time, but her thoughts kept whirling. The whole world was awaiting her decision—the whole world and then some! Not only were all of the living present, but all of the dead had come back as well. Everyone was there, including one guest whose presence is more important than all the others. And that guest is you, dear reader, without whom none of this would be happening.

As the waiting crowd became impatient, they surged forward. A tremendous roar of "Guilty!" filled the auditorium, followed by desperate cries of "Not guilty!"

Then, just as it looked as if Armageddon were happening for real, Mary took the microphone falteringly in her hands and said, "Actually, I don't think the verdict is 'guilty' or 'not guilty.' It's both and neither."

The crowd was shocked into absolute silence. So, with unaffected assurance, Mary poured out her heart, saying, "I've been on an incredible journey that has led me to this moment of decision. It's the journey of my life. There has been great joy and awful suffering. I've been exalted and humbled. I've loved it and hated it.

"I've been seduced and cajoled by life into accepting things as they are. I see now that they could be no other way, for life is the dance of duality—an eternal conversation between good and bad, yes and no, past and future. Life is the marriage of the mystery and the manifest, a love affair between Imagination and limitation. And love without pain isn't really romance. So how can I be bitter?

"Once I was lost in the limitations of life, but now I've stepped out into the endless possibilities. I struggled to know my own character until I realized that I was the Author. I listened to the voice of wisdom deep within me until I recognized that it was my own voice speaking. The nightmare of separateness has passed, and I've dissolved in the wonder of oneness.

"We play our individual roles in the drama of life, but I watch as all arises within the Primal Imagination that is our universal identity. The Author is all. So there's no one to blame and no one to praise. None are guilty; everyone is forgiven. I'm overwhelmed by a poignant love that embraces both friend and enemy.

"I appear to be Mary, but I am the Author. And you await my judgment, but I've had enough of judging. I feel only appreciation. I don't understand life, but I know I love being and I'm grateful for that.

"I am the mystery of Imagination within which this moment is arising, and I must decide what will happen next. So I'll tell you my deepest desire: I long for us to put aside enmity and be kind to each other. I yearn for us to come together as one and celebrate the miracle of existence. I want everyone to enjoy the story."

The equanimity of eternity filled the Great Court at the End of Time, and neither victims nor perpetrators said a word. Not a thought passed through their minds. Then Mary closed her eyes and whispered tenderly, "I am the Author speaking through Mary. But now, as I pronounce the Last Judgment, the moment has come when I will speak to each of you directly. . . ."

177

CHAPTER 28

Everyone heard the voice, but no one knew where it was coming from, until they realized that it was speaking inside their own mind. And although each person was hearing the same words, the voice that each person heard was their own.

The voice spoke with the wisdom of experience but not of one life only. The voice was as deep as the sea and infinitely sad; it was as bright as the sun and fresh as the morning. It was the voice of one who had suffered all that could be suffered and yet remained proud. It was the voice of one who had known the greatest victories yet was still humble. It was the voice, dear reader, of your own true Self.

And the voice said, "I love you."

Words can't describe what happened next. First, there was the sound of a mighty wind that seemed to sweep away the past as everyone exhaled a delicious sigh of relief. Then laughter began to rise from the depths, like a wave of joy from an ocean of bliss, pushing aside all animosity and acrimony.

And that was when the party started—the party to end all parties . . . the party at the End of Time.

CHAPTER 29

As Jesus, Mary, and Peter walked each other home the morning after—tired, but still smiling—the world seemed new. Colors were vibrant in the warm light of dawn; and birds sang a celebration of existence, flipping and twirling their cascading melodies like John Coltrane.

It seemed to Peter that he felt truly happy for the first time, and he whispered contentedly, "That was a big gig! I don't know what was in the water that Jesus turned into wine, but everyone had a wicked time."

"It was ecstasy," said Jesus. Then he added wryly, "I bet you never expected the Last Judgment would be such fun."

Mary couldn't resist a giggle of delight at the memory of it all. "Do you remember when the lights went down, the vibe came in, and the music got going? Low and ambient at first, building the anticipation. It seemed as if the entire world was whistling and cheering in expectation . . . and then—BAM! The kick drum hit the groove and the whole house started heaving."

"It was out of this world," said Jesus, taking one last toke on a jazz cigarette and passing it on to Peter.

"It was Heaven," said Peter, who was grinning so wildly that his jaw was aching. "They played my favorite song all night along."

And then, unable to restrain himself, he let out one more refrain from the slightly irritating acid-house anthem that he'd been requesting throughout the night: *"Acieed!"*

"And there wasn't a Christian soft-rock band in the lineup. Thank God!" bellowed Jesus overenthusiastically.

"The Devil has all the best tunes," agreed Peter. And then he added, *"Acieed!"*

"That really was the party at the End of Time!" enthused Mary. "Everyone was dancing like there was no tomorrow."

"The atmosphere was electric," agreed Jesus "It was like the classic raves in the Telesterion at Eleusis."

Mary couldn't contain the feeling of euphoria. "Do you remember when Paul came on and mashed it up with the Black Eyed Peas, extemporizing a rap based on that 'Big Love' passage from his Letter to the Corinthians—the one that always gets used at weddings and funerals?"

"Paul's the real deal!" announced Jesus.

"Shorty's very naughty!" added Mary.

"And then Bob bounced on and did 'One Love,'" reminisced Peter.

"I'll never forget watching Billy Graham and the Dalai Lama funking it up together in the strobe light," tittered Mary.

"That was messing with my melon, man!" acknowledged Peter.

"And then Zen master Dogen got the whole crowd chanting 'This Isness is the business!'" added Jesus. "Unbelievably cool!"

"They were all there," affirmed Mary. "Valentinus looked totally loved up; even Guru Nanak let his hair down—and man, does he have long hair!"

Then Peter shrieked, "And what about Pope Benedict coming on stage and throwing all his bling into the crowd, raving ecstatically about giving everything away to the poor?!"

"I couldn't help but find it funny," confessed Jesus. "Especially when Karl Marx joined him, shouting, 'We've nothing to lose but our chains!'"

And Mary declared, "Then on came that bunch of witches and Muslim women, calling themselves 'Girls Allowed,' doing the Dance of the Seven Veils to 'We Are Family'—wild or what?!"

Peter squealed with delight. "Then all those clergymen came out in front of everyone and sang 'Y.M.C.A.' with the Village People and pink petals fell like raindrops. Beautiful!"

Jesus wiggled with pleasure. "All of which was leading to the incredible climax of the show: when they lowered down that awesome gold cross with a seemingly lifeless figure crucified on it, who suddenly sprang into action as the night exploded with those mad Cubist fireworks that Picasso laid on."

"I must have missed that when I was in the restroom having a drink, because I was getting so dehydrated," replied Peter. "Who was on the cross?"

"Madonna, of course!" roared Jesus. "It was great to see an iconic woman up there on a cross instead of me for a change."

"What? Your old mom on a cross?" asked Peter in disbelief.

"No, no," explained Jesus, falling about in hysterics. "You know . . . Madge the Kabbalist."

"And just like a prayer, she took us there!" added Mary.

"That's totally blasphemous!" complained Peter in mock disgust. "Is nothing sacred?!"

"Not when everything is sacred," suggested Mary, and they all laughed.

Then Peter asked, "Did you make it into the chill-out space? It was smoldering in there."

"Most certainly, dude," replied Jesus. "Now that's what I call a love feast!"

Peter's smile was larger than the smile on the smiley-face T-shirt that he was now proudly wearing. Then he sniggered, "Did you see the look of panic and delight on the faces of Osama and George when they came 'round in the morning in each other's arms? Priceless!"

Jesus, Mary, and Peter looked at one another and beamed.

"It *was* good," said Peter.

"It *is* good," said Mary.

"It's *all* good," said Jesus.

And that was when Mary felt it would be fun to be serious for a moment, so she asked Jesus, "Was that *really* the Last Judgment?"

And the Lord replied, "When we finally hear our deepest being saying 'I love you' to our separate self, that's our very last judgment. Once we're in love, we're no longer judgmental."

"Did everyone hear the voice, Jesus?" asked Mary. Then she added, "Did you hear the voice, dear reader?"

And the Lord answered, "For a moment, we all heard what we've always longed to hear, and we realized that we're all one in love. We are all the Author of All, and the Author loves being each one of us."

"It was wonderful," said Mary solemnly. Then she added, "But will it last?"

"Probably not," conceded Jesus. "As they come to, most people will just go back to whatever state they call 'normal,' but that's okay. It's good to go back into the story—it's a fantastic story, after all!"

"There's no going back after an experience like that!" exclaimed Peter.

But Jesus answered, "We step out of the illusion of separateness in order to step back in as ambassadors of oneness."

Then he added conspiratorially, "And if that sounds too grand, we can simply become secret agents for love."

"All right," pronounced Mary. "Let's do it!"

And so it came to pass that Mary took Jesus and Peter by the arm and they skipped together down the yellow brick road . . . back into their story.

Rejoicing in the dawning of a brand-new day, they sang their hearts out with a passionate chorus of "Over the Rainbow"—interspersed with Peter throwing back his head and bellowing, *"Acieed!"*

CHAPTER 30

Eventually the Lord spoke, saying, "Well, guys, we've finally arrived at the last chapter."

"This book has more codas than a Beethoven symphony," exclaimed Peter.

"I can't quite believe we've been able to sustain this level of heresy for so long," quipped Mary.

"Surely there can't be many more buttons left to press," agreed Peter.

"I have to say it's been great fun mocking Literalist religion," confessed Mary.

"We've been milking those sacred cows for all they're worth," concurred Peter.

Then the Lord spoke with caution in his voice, saying, "The thing is, my dear comrades in the great work, we won't overturn religion by being rude about it. We need to offer a genuine alternative."

"But it's a good thing to lampoon religion, isn't it?" asked Mary. "It takes itself so damn seriously—it demands to be mocked."

"Oh yes," replied the Lord. "It's important to ridicule religion, but not *just* to ridicule it. I'm a both/and man myself."

Then he added, "We need to *both* poke fun at the past *and* to offer as an alternative a new version of the perennial Gnostic wisdom of love and oneness."

And Peter said, "I'm hoping the mix of postmodern parody and profound philosophy that we've been playing with in this gospel will help give Christianity the sort of makeover it so desperately needs. I mean, anyone can see it's been sagging horribly for centuries."

"Perhaps this gospel will help reconnect Christianity to its Gnostic roots?" suggested Mary optimistically.

"God forbid!" exclaimed Jesus. "The Gnostic Christians are interesting as a historical curiosity, but they're a bit passé now. Most of their gospels are pretty impenetrable, and some are as crazy as a coconut."

"You're right," conceded Mary. "All that stuff about archons and aeons doesn't really do it anymore."

And Peter added, "To be honest, that sort of nonsense never worked for me. Take that passage in the Gospel of the Egyptians where it goes: 'A hidden, invisible mystery came forth: iiiiiiiiiiiiiiiiiiiiii EEEEEEEEEEEEEEEEEEEEEE oooooooooooooooooooooooo uuuuuuuuuuuuuuuuuuuuuuu eeeeeeeeeeeeeeeeeeeeeee aaaaaaaaaaaaaaaaaaaaaaa OOOOOOOOOOOOOOOOOOOOOO.'"

"Yeah! What's all that about?" said Mary.

"It's bananas," agreed Jesus. "We don't need to go back to the past—the whole idea of 'ancient wisdom' is a bit of a fantasy, to tell you the truth. Just because someone's been dead for a long time doesn't mean they're any more insightful. Most of the dead people I know are idiots.

"We need to go forward, not back. Most important, we need a spirituality that embraces the life story, not one that encourages us to reject the world. No more scourging the body and denying ourselves the pleasures of the flesh.

"We need a philosophy that can help us wake up to oneness and enjoy the delights of separateness, so that we live fully, consciously uniting all that we are: Spirit, soul, and body."

And Mary said, "The problem is that the sort of people we really need to reach aren't likely to read a gospel like this. How do we communicate this wonderful wisdom beyond words to those lost in Literalism?"

And Peter smiled broadly and suggested, "Let's stand outside churches giving away leaflets saying:

"'Had enough of following the Christ?
Wanna be a Christ yourself?
Text BLASPHEMY 666.'"

"That's good," giggled Mary, enjoying the fact that Peter seemed to have developed a sense of humor at last. Then she added, quite seriously, "We need to communicate Jesus's perennial message in innovative ways. For example, do we really need yet another gospel? Books are old technology. Why not make a movie? Mel Gibson could play Peter."

"No more movies about Jesus!" exclaimed Jesus as the camera closed in on his piercing blue eyes, which strangely never blinked. "Enough is enough—the whole Jesus thing has to end here. It's time to lay the ultimate ghost to rest. I must be edited out of the story completely to make way for a new Gnosticism for a new age."

In the distance, an African choir began to softly sing a stirring gospel version of "Imagine"; and there was a beautiful cross-fade to a soft focus shot of Mary, her golden locks blowing in the breeze.

"You're right, Lord," she said, gazing heroically into the distance. And then she added, "As always."

The sound track swelled as a sumptuous string section supported the soaring sopranos and Mary cleared her voice for the visionary monologue she'd be rehearsing for weeks. Then, speaking directly to the camera, she began. . . .

"In my heart of hearts, I have sympathy for religious fundamentalists. The modern world offers nothing but crass consumerism, which will never satisfy the soul. People want more. Is it any surprise that they turn from the existential insecurities of secularism to the reassuring certainties of religion?"

Mary opened her arms theatrically, as if to embrace the whole world, and continued, "We need an alternative to superstition and supermarkets—we need a new faith to live by. Not faith in old books, but faith in the power of love to overcome all divisions. We need exactly the sort of profound ideas found in the philosophy section of this gospel."

Feeling on a roll, Mary threw back her head and proclaimed, "Deep down, we all long for paradise. That's because we're here to create Heaven on Earth: to bring our dreams of how good it could be into reality. And, perhaps, if enough of us could wake up to oneness, we could turn this whole thing around."

Mary took her voice down to a stage whisper to add to the emotional effect, saying, "Maybe we need just one more person to wake up, and the culture of cash will finally change into a culture of kindness."

She paused for as long as she could get away with, and then, with Shakespearean gravitas, delivered her final line: "Could that person be you, dear reader?"

As the background music climaxed with the final chorus of "Imagine," the editor did a neat cut to Jesus, who looked straight at the reader.

Then, deliberately garbling John Lennon's immortal lines to avoid copyright charges, the Lord said softly, "You see, my friend, I'm not the only dreamer. Perhaps some day you'll consider joining us—and the world will be a lot more fun."

A tear rolled down Peter's cheek and he closed his eyes to bathe in the intoxicating optimism of this glorious vision. As the music faded, Mary went back to gazing heroically into the distance; and a Technicolor sunset cast its vibrant light on the hill of Golgotha, where the gray silhouette of an empty cross gradually disappeared into the all-embracing night.

"Does that mean what I think it means?" asked Mary in a hushed voice.

"Yes," announced Jesus portentously. "The end is nigh."

"How exactly does this gospel end?" asked Peter off camera. "Do you and Mary move to the south of France and give birth to Leonardo da Vinci?"

"I'm returning now to the Primal Imagination from whence I arose," explained Jesus, "but I'll always be with you as a symbol of your true self: the Christ."

Mary gave a bittersweet smile, and Peter asked plaintively, "But what about me and Mary?"

"You'll live happily ever after," said Jesus warmly. "I can promise you that because this gospel is going to end with you two getting it on—and you'll be left there in love for all time."

Peter looked pleasantly surprised and Mary just looked surprised.

So Jesus added, "Remember that we're symbols of the self. I represent Spirit, Mary represents the soul, and Peter represents the body. Now that Mary is conscious of her deeper nature, she'll finally be able to love Peter, just as she has secretly always wanted to."

Mary let out an involuntary sigh and Peter asked excitedly, "Does that mean that *me and Mary* go to the south of France?"

Then Jesus spoke to them in prophecy, saying, "A wonderful fate awaits you. Through this Gospel of the Second Coming, you and Mary will inspire a new form of Gnostic spirituality, unfettered by the bane of Literalism that has kept us asleep in superstition for so long. This book will be the catalyst for an awakening that will transform the human adventure into a festival of love."

Mary took Peter tenderly by the hand and began to quietly blubber. The sound track returned with Sinatra singing "My Way" and Peter successfully managed to resist the temptation of singing along, which would have ruined the magic of the moment.

As Peter mouthed the words to the bit about "facing the final curtain," the camera turned to the lonely figure of the Lord, watching as the darkness consumed Golgotha and a clumsy group of extras dismantled an empty cross.

"That's that, then," said Jesus. And he smiled.

Mary began to sob quietly. "You're going now, aren't you?"

Jesus gave a parental "I know best" look and Peter asked, "Can you leave us a comforter or something?"

"The only true comforter is love," said Jesus. "I leave you with love—as much love as you can possibly contain. Omnipresent. Omnipotent. Very Big Love."

And then, with a mischievous wink to the reader, Jesus disappeared, just as your reflection does when you stop looking in the mirror.

Mary squeezed Peter's hand and whispered softly, "Let us live in imitation of the Lord, by also being conscious that we don't really exist."

Peter left a poignant pause to give the impression that he was seriously considering this possibility. Then he edged a little closer to Mary's warm body and asked, "How was the Second Coming for you, babe?"

And Mary replied in her mysterious voice, saying, "Don't ask that question of me; rather, ask it of the reader, because, dear reader, all that really matters is that Christ comes in you."

With this profound and vaguely autoerotic pronouncement reverberating in the reader's mind, Mary glanced back at Golgotha one last time as it faded into the past.

Then suddenly she spoke in astonishment, saying, "Hang on a minute!" And the background music screeched to an abrupt halt.

"Who's that crucified on either side of where Jesus's cross used to be?" asked Mary in astonishment.

"It's just those two crooks," reassured Peter, putting an arm around her.

"But look who it is," said Mary, pausing for dramatic effect. "It's Freke and Gandy!"

"Just when there was a chance of getting my leg over! What are those jokers doing here?"

"Try not to be judgmental, my darling," said Mary sweetly. "I know it's fitting that Freke and Gandy are playing the two thieves because they plagiarized most of their best ideas. But I can't help feeling sorry for them, stuck in such suffering of their own making. It's a sad sight—like some mongrel hybrid of a macabre Renaissance painting and the comic finale of the *Life of Brian*."

Peter looked concerned because he thought that was more likely to get him laid later. "I thought they were meant to be so wise?"

"You've obviously never met them. On their publicity blurbs they sound pretty impressive, but they're only wise when Christ speaks through them. The rest of the time they're decidedly average."

Then Mary looked deeply into Peter's eyes and added affectionately, "Just like you, my love."

And so it came to pass, just as Jesus had prophesied, that Peter and Mary finally kissed—a full-bodied, passionate, tongue-in-mouth kiss. (And the first one that Peter hadn't had to pay for.)

The sentimental background music began to swell once more, with a poignant country-and-western treatment of "Always Look on the Bright Side of Life," featuring some haunting slide guitar. The credits rolled and the camera slowly panned to rest on two forlorn figures, crucified on either side of a missing cross.

Freke grinned at Gandy, who groaned and shifted his weight to a different nail.

"Are you finding this funny, mate?"

"Don't start on all that Laughing Jesus crap again."

"Give us a smile, you old bugger."

"What? On these royalties?!"

"Maybe this book will actually sell enough copies to warrant the huge effort it's taken to write?"

"That's what you say every time."

"Well, at least our theory about Jesus not existing turned out to be right—Jesus said so himself."

"Being right doesn't pay the bills."

"What about Mary's idea of making this book into a movie? Movies make money. We should end with that in mind."

"Why do you think we're closing with this parody of Monty Python? That's a parody of a parody. How postmodern is that?!"

"I hope this gospel hasn't offended too many people—I hate upsetting anyone."

"It's a bit late to worry about that!"

"I suppose now that we've gotten rid of God, there's not much point in praying that someone will get us out of this mess?"

"What I want to know is how our agent didn't notice the clause that Jesus slipped in the contract about him skipping off and us ending up here."

"Yeah! I never agreed to that. What a slippery fish."

"So are we going to resurrect or hang about forever?"

"I guess we'll be stuck here as long as we believe that we're the authors of this book."

ACKNOWLEDGMENTS

Timothy Freke and Peter Gandy would like to acknowledge the support of all those who helped make the publication of this manuscript possible, including Deborah O'Shea-Freke, Becky Wright of New Leaf, Mary Anderson, Jefferson Glassie and Julie Littell of Peace Evolutions LLC, George Kuhn, Marlene Carpenter, Craig Green, Agnieszka Buczek, Tina Bass, Phil Campbell, Bernard F. Pracko II, Mark Aelred of Circle of the Free Spirit, Monica and Michael Stafford, Paul Herwerp, and especially Theo Simon of Seize the Day for his invaluable creative and editorial input.